CHARLIE GRAY

The Frog No More

A Zany Observation of Sober Life

gray house

First published by Gray House 2023

Copyright © 2023 by Charlie Gray

All rights reserved. No part of this publication may be reproduced, stored or transmitted in any form or by any means, electronic, mechanical, photocopying, recording, scanning, or otherwise without written permission from the publisher. It is illegal to copy this book, post it to a website, or distribute it by any other means without permission.

Charlie Gray asserts the moral right to be identified as the author of this work.

The following is a true account of my childhood, teenage years, adulthood, and my struggle with addiction and identity. To maintain their anonymity, some names have been changed. Actual names of individuals or names of treatment centers were used with express written permission.

First edition

ISBN: 979-8-9871879-5-1

Cover art by Euan Monaghan
Illustration by Eva Polakovicova

This book was professionally typeset on Reedsy.
Find out more at reedsy.com

For You

Contents

Preface ii
Acknowledgement iii
  1 The End's Beginning 1
  2 Bucksaw Point Resort & Marina 4
  3 Antioch 29
  4 Loss of Innocence 40
  5 A Colosseum Shit Demon 57
  6 Wine, Cigs, & Feathers 68
  7 Adrift & Running Amok 77
  8 Spun for Fun 90
  9 Affinity 97
10 Klaus the Savior 115
11 Wenches & Trollops Take Europe 128
12 To 2023 & Beyond! 145
About the Author 161
Also by Charlie Gray 162

Preface

As I conclude my zany memoir trilogy, I hope these pages have provided a means of comfort and escape for any and all touched by addiction. I hope to create reassurance through my tales, written for those struggling to wade amid trying times. I wish you the best and send my love.

And now, I present the story of the evolution of my addiction, observed in sobriety.

Acknowledgement

Thank you very much for coming along on this journey with me! Believe me, it could not have been accomplished without your support. A special thanks to the following:

My Family, *thank you for your love, support, and grace.*
My Friends, *thank you for never giving up on me!*
Klaus, *my best furry friend! Thanks for keeping me sane!*
Devin, *thank you for standing by my side since The Dawn of The Fanny.*
Mallorie, *thank you ever so much for always bringing joy and light into my life.*
B. William, *thank you for being you—you have inspired me more than you could ever know.*
Cory, Ransom, & Castro, *my favorite boys ever, my jolly comrades! I love you all so much!*
Chrissy, *thank you for your continued support and encouragement!*
Euan & Eva, *thank you for helping bring The Frog to life!*
Online Sober Community, *thank you for your guidance and I love you all!*

1

The End's Beginning

October 2022
Clinton, Missouri
36 Years Old

Slumped against an enormous oak tree, I smile fondly as a gentle breeze rustles the fallen leaves, scattering them over the sunny meadow to float upon a tiny pond, tucked away and hidden by the verdant woods. The forest is silent, save for the chatter of birds and squirrels, an occasional falling walnut, or the snap of a twig. It is a space of complete tranquility, and during each visit, I vow to spend more time relaxing beneath its shade, a vow I do not honor as faithfully as I should.

As far back as I can remember, I have always found immense comfort and security from sitting in the woods, quietly and alone. I am a "Son of the Forests," for they allow me the capability to become entirely lost in myself. I release the tensions and concerns of everyday life and candidly listen to the wants and needs of my soul. Spending quality alone time in nature has proved to be a vital ingredient to my sustained sobriety, as well.

If only I had known of its restorative magic sooner!

Oh, that's honestly a silly thought, for I have always known of its restorative powers, I simply chose to ignore that guidance when it stood between me and the almighty vodka bottle. Because I *wanted* the bottle, above anything else. I can see that now, I can understand and accept that about myself *now*. At the time, however, I was only able to understand it in a cerebral sense. My mind understood my behavior, yet it had trouble communicating that information with my heart. There was a severe disconnect between my head and my heart, a disconnect fueled by my shame and fear. But how does one see this about oneself in the throes of active addiction? How does one pause their life to view it objectively? To this day, I have no idea how one would go about accomplishing that feat during active addiction. It was not a skill I developed. Although, with the aid of many therapists, rehabs, and a pinch of patience, I learned to establish a connection between my head and heart *during* sobriety; I made a daring decision to face my past during a rare moment of sober clarity, and it saved my life.

How?

I reconnected with the boy of my youth, finding similarities with the man I am today, and in doing so, discovered my authentic self. I dismissed the notion of shame and embraced the perfectly imperfect man I am, which turned out to be much easier than I anticipated.

Over these last few weeks, I have taken time to reflect on my life and gather a few takeaways. It all began with an endearing daydream depicting a montage of my younger self: a white-haired boy hyperactively zooming up and down the steep ramp of Bucksaw Resort, writing poems about ashes, and acting out dramatic, impromptu monologues on the docks of our marina. I was a carefree, affable, curious, and slightly melodramatic kid, utterly unaware of how these traits would serve me in the future.

I'd never viewed my life as a journey—to me, it seemed to be a series of random events. Perhaps it was a classic case of being unable to see the forest for the trees? More likely, I wasn't ready to define my life in such a way. I wasn't equipped with the insight to "chapter" it out, to connect the dots, to notice patterns and precedents. I had yet to stumble across the epiphany that alcohol has been a constant in my life since I was ten years old. Even in recovery, as I abstained from drinking, alcohol disillusioned me with its wicked power. For years, I convinced myself I was in my early twenties before I began to abuse alcohol, when in fact, my drinking was much like that of an alcoholic by the tender age of *thirteen*. And I don't feel I was *meant* to be aware of this information until now, either. Please understand, this is not to suggest I have reached absolute enlightenment—far from it—merely that I finally understand these bones and this soul. I met him on the battlefield of life, my gracious savior amidst a war of chaos. It seems the melodrama has stuck with me, eh?

In all seriousness, the greatest gift of sobriety has come from embracing my past, which has allowed for a deeper understanding of its purpose in leading me to where I stand today. I would not be able to write of my trials and tribulations were it not for many experiences and opportunities along the way, both good and bad. And it was in learning the value and lessons of these experiences and opportunities that I found my salvation.

Let me clarify.

My journey sharpened me. I have learned to navigate the rocky terrain of life, rather than having it cast me hither and thither. Once I employed the power of my mind and accepted that life was not happening to me, but happening with me, by me, and for me, equanimity settled over me. I achieved grace. This was the ultimate piece in my gigantic, confusing, and draining sobriety puzzle. My appetite for life was reborn, and I yearned to share my story as a means of comfort for those struggling with a similar plight.

My emotional renaissance spilled over me as quickly as a spreading fire, although I could not conceive its full extent until recently. I had spent so many years waiting for my "moment of surrender," I didn't give it much thought other than *finally*! Yet, after a couple of years in recovery, I continue to find myself touched by its ripple effects. It never ceases to amaze me, and I hope that by providing my life and journey as an example, I may help others to find the same enjoyment and purpose in living I have found.

With a grin blooming across my face, I stand and stretch.

"Welp, I'm fairly sure you just sorted out what you'd like to do with your third book, chap," I say under my breath, happiness rising in my chest.

2

Bucksaw Point Resort & Marina

Summer 1996
Tightwad, Missouri
10 Years Old

Early morning sun bursts over the jagged cliffs, golden light spilling onto the placid waters of Truman Lake and reflecting through our balcony door. A refreshing summer breeze stirs the air, rocking the marina ever so slightly, its thick and gnarly anchoring wires swaying gracefully inches above the lake's surface. Colorful birds dive from the bright blue morning sky, squawking and flapping around the docks for discarded fish and minnows. Boat engines roar dully, pierced by the shouts of a dock hand or the giggling shrieks of a kid. The smell of bacon and toast wafts from the restaurant below our apartment, and my stomach rumbles noisily.

This is my favorite time of day. I love waking up with the sunrise, quietly tip-toeing down the hall and out the front door to the restaurant's kitchen below, grabbing a snack, and then sprinting up the ramp, across the gravel parking lot, bounding the broad wooden steps up the hill, and jumping into the pool cannonball-style.

Like most mornings, Dad is already downstairs, directing boats and fishing guides, and Brod will sleep with Mom for a couple more hours. This is the ideal time of day for exploring the forest around the resort, as well, but today

I will swim! I ventured around the woods for hours yesterday and was eaten alive by mosquitoes. I need to spend the day floating, gazing at the clouds, and soaking my mosquito bites in the chlorine of the pool.

"You can play with those rings if you want to, I don't mind. They sink and then you can dive down and get them, or pick them up with your toes! That's fun, too!" I say to a little girl in a metallic blue swimsuit. Her short brown hair clings to her face as she wades in the shallow end of the pool.

"See, like this."

I toss the blue, orange, and green rings into the deep end, peering over the pool's edge as they float to the bottom. She stares at me without moving, her green eyes curious.

"Too deep?" I shrug. "It's okay. Do you want to play with them in the shallow end? That's where my little sister likes to play with them."

"She's shy," a girl's voice echoes from inside the poolhouse.

"Oh," I say, startled. She walks through one of the many sliding glass doors, taller than the girl in the pool, but with the same green eyes and brown hair. "Is she your baby sister?"

"Yeah," the taller girl answers, stepping from the shadows of the poolhouse.

"Cool! I have a baby sister, named Brodie. My name is Charlie, and this is my resort. What're your names?"

"I'm Mary Jane and that's Mona," Mary Jane answers, walking down the wooden steps of the poolhouse.

"Hello, nice to meet you, Mary Jane and Mona," I smile.

Mona grins back at me and then scurries from the pool to her big sister.

"What do you mean, this is your resort?" Mary Jane asks, sitting daintily on the pool steps and delicately dipping her feet into the water.

"Well, my grandparents built it before I was born, and now my dad and mom own it. And my aunts and uncles work here, too, and I live above the tackle shop and restaurant. You see that word 'restaurant' on the marina?" I point.

Mary Jane cranes her neck around a pair of decorative bushes and nods.

"Now see that window beside it? That's my house," I beam.

THE FROG NO MORE

"You *live* on top of the *water?*" Mary Jane gapes.

"Yup!" I say with delight.

One of my favorite things in the entire world is to tell people I live in a house that floats on the water. Well, I guess it's technically a very spacious apartment, but I don't think that matters much.

"Wow!" Mary Jane marvels while Mona peers at the two of us with wonder. "And you can go swimming anytime you want?"

"Yup! Well, when the pool's open and the lake's warm. We have to close the pool in the winter, but the hot tub stays open! It's great!"

"I bet it is!" Mary Jane agrees.

"So, where are you two from?" I ask, easing my way down the steps of the pool.

"We're from Mayfield, Kentucky. Dad's here to fish in the tournament, so we rented a cabin."

"Oh? Which cabin are you in?"

Mary Jane's eyebrows pinch together as she thinks. "Six. Yeah, it's the last one."

"Really? That's one of my favorites! Cabin one and cabin six are the best ones!" I gush. "How old are you?"

"I'm nine, and Mona is four," Mary Jane says, splashing her feet.

"I just turned ten, and my sister is three. She's up at the lodge with my mom and Aunt Trella right now, but she'll probably want to come down and swim later."

Mary Jane glances at the lodge behind us, high up on the hill and overlooking the entirety of the resort.

"Huh," she clucks. "Do you have a boat?"

"My mom has a speed boat and my granny has a pontoon. Grandpa John has a couple of fishing boats, but I like the pontoon the best. It has a hard top roof, so you can climb the ladder and sit on top of it. I love to lay up there at night and look at the stars."

"That sounds so cool! Wow! Um, do you have to go to school?" Mary Jane inquires as if I'm from another planet.

"Of course I go to school, silly. It's not even that far from here, really," I say simply, diving beneath the water and swimming the length of the pool. I clasp the ledge of the deep end and pull myself to a sitting position, waving at Mary Jane and Mona on the other side of the pool.

"What happens if it floods?" Mary Jane hollers.

"The marina rises with the water. A couple of years ago it flooded so bad you couldn't even see the parking lot. The water almost made it up to here, up to the pool. We had to take boats to get from the marina to the lodge, it was so cool!" I giggle, remembering. Mary Jane's eyes are wide. "But it was fine by the winter. The parking lot was back. Santa Claus even came and walked down it!"

"Santa?" Mona repeats reverently.

"*What?*" Mary Jane squeals. "Santa Claus came to *this* parking lot? Did he have his reindeer and sleigh?"

"No," I laugh. "It was just him, walking down the parking lot and waving. Brod was too little to know what was going on, but I stood at the window, that one I showed you, and watched the whole thing. I was beginning to doubt if Santa Claus was actually real, you know, but then I saw him walking down *our* parking lot and could have kicked myself for doubting!"

"Wow," Mary Jane bows her head, then looks up at me with a frown. "You're a lucky kid, you know that?"

"Yeah, getting to see Santa Claus was so lucky!" I nod.

"No, not just that. Look at where you live. And you said your whole family works here?"

"Yeah, my Aunt Trella and Uncle Tom live up at the lodge."

"And you get to swim all day and go out on boat rides whenever you want. Why *wouldn't* Santa Claus visit you? Who wouldn't want to visit the *luckiest* kid in the world?"

A strange sensation tugs at my stomach, tension clouding the air. Mary Jane doesn't sound friendly or happy anymore; she sounds sad and mad. Did I say something wrong? I offered to share my toys with Mona, and I'll share them with her, too.

"You can play with those rings, too, if you want," I say, standing. "Or I've got a bunch of other toys in the poolhouse, downstairs. I can go down there and get them."

"More toys?" Mary Jane repeats softly.

"Yeah, you want me to go get them?"

"No. I'm not wearing my swimsuit, and we should probably get back to the cabin."

"Oh. Well, okay. Brod and I will be swimming later today if you want to come back. Brod's got all kinds of things for little kids, too, Mona," I say.

Mary Jane pulls her feet from the water and motions to Mona. "Come on, Mona. Let's go see if Mom needs our help with anything."

Mona looks from Mary Jane to me, then reluctantly takes Mary Jane's hand. I stand at the deep end and wave them goodbye.

"Bye, Mary Jane and Mona!" I cheese.

"Bye, luckiest boy in the *world*!" Mary Jane zings.

Later that night, I snuggle beside my mom on our squishy green leather couch, watching a rerun of *Friends*. She sits with her legs crossed, bouncing one foot gently.

"Mom?" I ask.

"Yeah, babe?" she murmurs.

"I think something happened at the pool today—nothing bad—I was just talking to a couple of other kids, and one of them kept calling me the luckiest boy in the world." I pull away from her, resting against the cushions. "But it made me feel bad, for some reason," I frown.

"Well, what were y'all talking about?"

"Just about the marina, and living here, and swimming, and how Santa Claus walked down the parking lot. And she asked if I had a boat, and I told her about your speed boat and Granny's pontoon."

"Well, honey, some kids don't have boats. Or a swimming pool they can go to whenever they want. Some kids don't have as many places to play and have fun. Some kids have a much different childhood than you have, and you *are* very lucky for that. But what probably happened was that hearing all those great things made her sad. And sometimes when people are sad, they can be hurtful and mean."

"Because *they're* hurting?"

"Exactly," Mom says, wrapping her arm around me. "Exactly, babe."

"It makes me sad that Mary Jane is sad, Mom," I realize.

"Oh, babe, that is very kind of you, to be so understanding, but you worry about *yourself*, hun. You be the nice, caring boy I know you are, and everything will be just fine." She pats my head lovingly and I settle against her again, warm and secure in her embrace.

*****

Music thumps from the poolhouse, multi-colored strobe lights flashing through the sliding glass doors as people dance and mingle. I crouch behind an azalea bush a few yards from the entrance of the pool, hiding to watch the crowd dance, talk, and laugh. Trish and Mom's faces weave throughout the reveling, busting a move and throwing their heads back in laughter. My Aunt Dena twirls merrily on the small stage, her hand extended to my Uncle Chris.

I pout and huff, angry I'm considered "too little" to attend the party. I'm not too little to haul the trash cart up the ramp or help wait tables! I'm not too little to clean the cabins or babysit Brod and my cousins when they come to stay! I'm not too little when they actually *need* me!

Dang it, dang it, dang it!

"Too little!" I hiss, crossing my arms over my chest.

A shriek of giggles pierces the thunderous music and I turn my back on the party, bitter. Fine! I don't even want to see it. I'll roam the hill and the woods behind the lodge in the dark. Maybe I'll go on my own midnight adventure, and stay gone until tomorrow afternoon! That'll show them!

Except wait—werewolves! No, scratch that, they might bite me, or eat me! Mom was right, I never should have watched *Wolf*, but I love Catwoman and The Joker, my favorite villains from the *Batman* movies. Fine, I'll sneak back home and sulk in my room. Maybe I'll play a game on my computer to make myself feel better?

"Yeah, that sounds like a good idea," I decide, carefully crawling from behind the bush and scurrying down the hill. I am mindful to stay in the shadowy parts of the parking lot and zip down the ramp fast as lightning. In the safety of my room, I fire up my computer and catch my breath. Maybe I can't party tonight, but one day I won't be "too little" anymore, and I will party all the time!

"I'll throw so many fun, exciting parties, and *everyone* will be invited!" I declare to my empty room. "I'll be the best party monster there ever was!"

*****

Dad holds my hand as we tread the cracked and broken sidewalk of an old apartment complex, steering me to the entrance. A foul scent of grease and stale kitty litter greets us as he opens the door. Children scurry down the long hallway, a roach stuck to the stained wall, its uncovered lightbulbs flickering on and off. I gape around the space, overwhelmed by the sights and smells.

"Do you wanna play?" asks a child from a darkened doorway, wearing dirty shorts and a torn shirt. His eyes are wide and sunken.

I crane up at my dad, fearful.

"No, sorry, little man, he's got to say with me," Dad answers, resting his hands on my shoulders.

I breathe a sigh of relief as my dad leads me down the hallway and out of a doorway on the other end. Fresh air and sunlight welcome us.

"What *was* that place, Dad?" I exclaim in a hushed tone.

"Those are apartments I'm thinking about buying. They haven't been taken care of by the current owner, so they would need a lot of work before we could put them on the market, but they're actually in a fairly decent location, and salvageable."

"But how can people live there? There were so many bugs and it smelled really bad!" I balk.

"That's all some people can afford, son. It's the best they can do. And they're lucky, if you think about it, because they have a roof over their heads, heat in the winter, and air conditioning in the summer. Some people are a lot worse off," he pats my shoulder, assessing the exterior of the building and taking us back to his white Suburban.

Crawling up the running board and into the passenger seat, I fold my arms over my chest, a strange feeling churning in my chest.

"I think I understand what Mom was saying the other night. Some kids just have it rough, and that's life. You have to make the best of what you have, I guess," I shrug.

Dad grins at me from the driver's seat, a twinkle in his eye. "You saw a tough way of living today, and that is exactly right, Bub. Some kids are more fortunate than others, but it's up to us to make the best of what we've got. And, like *my* dad always said, if we want more in life, then we're going to have to work hard to get it, but it'll be worth it."

I nod, staring out the window as my dad zooms down the highway, the tall buildings of downtown Kansas City turning to the pastures of Peculiar. Dusk washes over the sky, the first evening stars twinkling brightly.

"Dad, does the universe ever end?" I ask, my eyes fixed on a faraway star.

"I don't think so. I think it goes on and on, but you should probably double-check that in your encyclopedias."

"It just goes on and on?" I turn to him, awestruck.

"I *think* so," he answers thoughtfully.

"So, the universe never ends?" I whisper in wonderment. "And we've only been to the moon? That means there could be all kinds of people out there. Well, aliens, I guess—not people. But who knows? Maybe there *are* people, too! Wow, Dad, I think I'm having my mind blown today."

He tosses his head back, chuckling. "Yeah?"

"Yeah! It really makes you wonder, doesn't it? Like, if the universe never ends, then how can we know if we're right about God and stuff? How can we know if we're right about *anything*? Because why would God make life so hard for some kids? Why would He do that? It makes me feel weird when I think about it, kinda like when you're on a roller coaster and your stomach feels like it's flying, you know? Like I can't catch my breath or something."

"You know I'm no fan of roller coasters, buddy, but I think I know what you mean."

"It's kinda scary," I admit.

"Ah, don't be scared. You're growing up, and part of growing up means you're going to have bigger thoughts. You're going to think about things you've never thought of before. But that's great—that's excellent! Never be scared of your own mind," he says.

I pinch the rubber handle of the door, thoughts swirling in my head.

"Dad, is God real? I mean, is He really *God*? Did He create all of this? The universe that never ends?"

Dad tilts his head sideways and chews on his bottom lip, his eyes focused on the road ahead. Religion has never been a main focus in our house, and I can tell he is truly weighing my question.

"I think God is real. I know He was with me when I wrecked my truck. I felt Him, and saw and felt things I'd never felt before. I don't think there's any other way to explain what happened to me other than God was there that day. He was with me, and I knew I was going to be okay."

"Did He talk to you?" I ask excitedly.

"Not really. It was more like a sense of peace, knowing He was there, that He was taking care of me, and that I would be alright. It was *very* peaceful."

"Hmm," I say. "I like that. Sometimes when people talk about God, they seem very angry, and they yell and use words like damnation. It confuses me, I don't know why there has to be so much anger with God."

"There's just a lot of anger in the world, babe," Dad sighs. "But don't let that worry you. You just keep having fun, you keep enjoying life. You're very good at that."

"I *am* very good at having fun," I agree. "Very good."

*****

I burrow under my favorite flannel blanket, nestled amid a pallet of quilts before the giant TV in the back corner of the restaurant. After a bit of coaxing, I was able to convince Mom to let me watch *Interview with the Vampire*, and I grin in glee at the opening credits. Little does she know this is actually my second time watching the movie, for I sneaked it to my room a few nights ago and watched it in the darkness of the early morning hours while everyone was still asleep.

I am fascinated with vampires. They thrill and excite me, and frighten me to death. Imagine living forever, young and beautiful, traveling the world! Gazing at the full moon with long, luscious hair! Yes, I am absolutely *obsessed* with vampires, and I will most certainly dress as one for Halloween this year. Maybe even Armand himself!

Trella's footsteps sound as she rounds the half-wall separating the tackle shop from the restaurant.

"Right on! You hanging down here with us while we paint?" she asks, chipper as ever.

Mom and Trella are capitalizing on the slow weekend by painting the ceiling tiles of the tackle shop and restaurant. Occasionally, we have an "off weekend," as we're usually hosting fishing tournaments that run almost continuously from mid-March to mid-October.

"Yup, Mom said I could watch *Interview with the Vampire* while y'all work and paint," I say avidly.

"Oh, wow, you like that movie?" she giggles.

"I love it! I think I love it more than *Pretty Woman*," I say in awe.

"Now *that's* saying something!" Trella balks.

"I know!" I agree. "*Pretty Woman* has been my favorite for years!"

"Years and years! Well, enjoy your vampires. We're gonna start in the tackle shop and work our way back to the restaurant."

I nod and turn back toward the TV, watching Louis talk with the interviewer. While I do like Louis and Lestat, I am *madly in love* with Armand and wish he and Louis would kiss at the movie's end. It is a beautiful, tragic love story, and for whatever reason, I understand it. It reminds me of the love story in *The Secret Garden* between Mary and Dickon. I am always swept away by their look of passion on the swing in the garden. I completely understand their hesitation to kiss, as if acting on the passion would tarnish the moment, cheating it of its potency. I'm not sure *why* I feel these things, I just do. They're simply there, like any other feeling. My "deep swells of adult emotions," I call them.

I wonder if Mom and Trella know I'm in love with Armand? I wonder if they would even care. *I* know that I am gay, and I know it's scary to be

THE FROG NO MORE

gay. I know a lot of gay men die from a mysterious disease I don't fully understand. A disease talked about with hushed tones and sad, downcast eyes. Something about Uncle Bradley, and his partner? I never seem to get any more information than that, though.

But *I'm* not afraid to be gay. And I'm not mad or sad about being gay, either. To me, being gay is no different than having blond hair or blue eyes; it's a small part of who I am. But I also understand the world at large does not always feel this way, and *that* makes me sad and mad. What are those song lyrics, though? *The times are changing*. Something like that.

"Oh, Charlie!" Mom gasps, grimacing from the bar at the front of the restaurant. "That's kinda morbid—is he drinking that chicken's blood? I don't remember him doing that in the book, but maybe he did."

"There's a book?" I spring from my pallet, bounding to where she stands.

"Yup, there's a book, I read it years ago. There are *several* books."

"Have you read them all?" I ask.

"Not all of them, but most of them."

"Who writes them?"

"Anne Rice," she says, popping open a can of navy-blue paint.

"I like that name!" I declare. "Do you have those books upstairs?"

"I think so, but you're a bit young to read them."

"I'm watching the movie, aren't I?" I retort slyly.

She fixes me with a steely stare, then shakes her head with a snicker. "Yes, you are. But what I mean is the books are full of large words and they're longer than your chapter books. They might confuse you, babe. Give it a couple more years and I'm sure you'll be ready to read them," she pats my head.

"But I want to read them *now*!" I sulk. "I want to know more about Louis' adventures, and Armand!"

"They're more about Lestat than Louis," she muses, stirring the paint.

"I wish there was more on Armand," I say casually.

"Oh, I'm sure she'll write one, eventually."

"Can I *please* read the book *Interview with the Vampire*? Please, Mom?" I plead, gripping the edge of the bar and swinging on it with my arms.

"Now you want to read the book, too?" Trella chortles, standing on a ladder and painting the ceiling of the tackle shop.

"Oh, my macabre child," Mom sighs with a grin. "Fine, yes. But I don't know where it's at right at this moment, so can you settle for the movie right now?"

I launch myself from the bar, flying over the linoleum entryway of the restaurant and landing on the carpet in peals of laughter.

"Yes! I can wait for the books! Thank you, Mom! I love you and I love books and I love vampires!"

*****

Mom stands behind the steering wheel of her green and white speed boat, wind whipping her platinum blonde ponytail as we tear across Truman Lake. I adjust my sunglasses and stretch out on the front seats, tiny splashes of water misting my chest and legs. Brod sits at the tip of the front, facing the wind, beaming and laughing in the face of danger as she clutches the edges of the upholstered seats. Trella rests in the co-captain chair, her feet propped on the windshield.

"Sit back, Brod!" Mom hollers.

Brod falls back squealing with giggles and makes eye contact with me. Oh, my little daredevil sister! My little sister who has no fear! Why, just last week, we raised ourselves fifty feet into the air using the boat lift straps, our legs dangling while we gawked around the lake, marina, and cliffs. Mom and Dad have no idea we play on that machinery, and we aim to keep it that way.

I stick my tongue out at Brod, fold my arms behind my head, and gaze at the cloudless sky. The early days of summer are the *best* days of summer, spent sunbathing and swimming in the lake with my family. "Easy days," I call them. Mom will drive us to Clinton Cove or further down to a smaller cove, thin and hidden, and Brod and I will swim to the shoreline in search of rare stones. We'll bob up and down in floaties and munch on snacks while Mom and Trella tan on the long front seats of her boat. My family spends the majority of the summer working on the resort, and these rare "off days" are a treat.

Mom slows the boat, twisting the wheel to maneuver a thicket of dead, lake-worn trees, their bark and limbs weathered and smoothed by the constant lapping of water. I reach my hand out and grip a thin, waterlogged tree as we float along, wiggling it.

"Has anyone seen the bald eagle lately?" I ask.

"Not this summer," Trella answers sadly, standing to apply tanning oil as we sail through the trees. "I think she took her babies and moved somewhere else last fall. I sure hope they're all okay."

"I wonder why she left?" I remark.

"She probably moved to a spot on the lake with fewer people," Mom says. "She wasn't able to get much peace in her nest. Everyone was always driving up to see her in it, especially after she had her babies. Poor thing."

"Oh, I bet she found the perfect tree somewhere, hidden away and cozy!" I beam.

"I bet you're right, Bub!" Trella agrees.

I jump on top of my seat in excitement, fling my arms open wide, and lose my balance. Gasping with fright, my body tips over the side of the boat, and my head bangs against a tree as I crash into the warm water. My shoulder bounces off the bottom of the boat and I kick my legs ferociously toward the surface before the current of the deeper waters traps me. My head breaks the surface and Trella's hands clasp my arms tightly as she yanks my torso out of the lake.

"Are you okay?" she screeches, my mom's eyes bulging in shock over her shoulder.

"Yeah," I cough, wiping my face.

"Bub!" Brod yelps tearfully.

"I'm okay," I say.

Mom and Trella scoop me into the boat and wrap me in a fluffy yellow towel.

"Brod, guess what?" I sputter. "I think I saw The Little Mermaid down there! She winked at me, waved, and then swam away!"

"You hit your head pretty hard, huh?" Mom chuckles, rubbing my shoulders and arms fiercely despite the warm temperature.

"I did hit my head, but The Little Mermaid was definitely down there. I know it—I saw *her*!" I proclaim vigorously.

"Okay, I believe you!" Mom smiles. "You still up for swimming? Do you feel okay?" she asks, holding my chin, staring into my eyes, and turning my head from side to side.

"Yeah, I'm okay. The Little Mermaid was with me, I'm all good," I shrug.

"You're such a little rock star," she grins.

*****

"Whoa there, buddy!" Hector warns as I zip around the counter of the tackle shop, diving for a piece of bubblegum. "Watch out for those fishing lures!"

"Yikes! They almost got me! That could have been bad."

"Right?" he chuckles. "What're you in such a hurry for?"

Hector is Bucksaw's youngest dockhand and one of my favorites. He's tall and skinny, with sandy brown hair and big teeth, and spends most of his time washing off the docks and pontoons, and manning the cash register. I think he is one of the funniest, coolest people on the planet, and enjoy being sent on adventures with him to clear brush and pick up trash off the shore of the lake.

"Well, the lake's way down. Water levels are awful this year, you know," I say breezily, shrugging. "And I figure it's up to me to bring on the rain. I'm gonna go up on the hill, by the well house, and talk to the clouds. I shall summon the rain!" I yelp, striking a goofy pose and sticking out my tongue.

"Like a rain dance?" Hector smiles.

"No, Hector, nothing like a rain dance! I can't do rain dances, I'm not Native American, I don't know how! So, I have to ask. I have to take a sacred offering, and ask nicely."

"Ah, and the gum is your sacred offering, huh?" he says reverently.

"Of course! Who doesn't love bubblegum?" I beam, grabbing a piece for myself and a piece for the rain gods.

"Sounds like an excellent idea, little buddy," he pats my shoulder. "But be careful. There's a lot going on this weekend. Slow down and watch where you're going, alright?" he reminds me kindly.

"Sure thing, Hector. You wanna come with me?"

"Nah, I better stay here and man the ship."

"Sounds good!" I holler, skipping out the door of the tackle shop and up the ramp.

It is a hot, sticky day, and I head directly for a shaded area of trees near the well house, smacking on bubblegum as I stride along.

After my conversation with Dad, God has been on my mind quite frequently. I'm still unsure of what to believe and asked Granny Norma Jean to take me to church last Sunday, but I ended up falling asleep during the service. I had trouble understanding what the preacher was talking about, and once Granny started scratching my head and playing with my hair, I was out like a light.

I want answers about God, though. I want to understand why He would let so many people suffer and die in pain, especially kids. I want to understand why I should blindly follow a faith that seems judgmental and cold to those who aren't "normal." I want to understand why a stab of fear and guilt pierces me when I think of Brandon, and how cute he is. I want to understand *why* God would say that is wrong—that I'm wrong for thinking these thoughts or having these feelings. Isn't He supposed to be the one who made them in the first place? I don't understand God, but I want to. I want explanations beyond "have faith" and "the Devil's tempting tricks."

I want to know why there are other Gods, and why some are viewed as fables, while others are viewed as opponents of God. There are *so many* Gods, and each one is different, and everyone seems fiercely protective of their God; they damn other Gods, and say their God is the only "one true way," and "one true faith," but with everyone screaming the same thing, how am I supposed to figure it out?

I find it much easier to talk with Mother Earth and the sky, thanking them for the sunshine and trees, and asking for rain. It is so much easier to gaze at the clouds in the sky, thanking them for their beauty and shade.

Coming to a halt under a pair of old maple trees, I peer at the cloudless, powder-blue sky and unwrap the second piece of bubblegum. Pinching it between my fingers, I raise my arms to the sky and steady my stance.

"I am confused by you, God, but that's the simplest name to call you, so I will call you that. I know I haven't been to church all that much or read the Bible. But I guess I should really apologize to *all* the Gods—I've never read *any* of your books. And I've only been to a couple of churches a few times. So, I'm sorry for that, and from now on I'll say Gods, since I have no idea which one of you is right or real. Maybe I should read your books, to find some answers, but I don't know. Some people who read your books do the most horrible things. Maybe I *shouldn't* read your books!

"See why I'm confused? Anyways, back to the point. The way I see it, I think you're everywhere. I think you're everything. But what I can't understand, what I have trouble with, is that *if* you're everywhere and everything, why do you let so much pain and sadness happen to those who don't deserve it? When I think of that, it seems to me that you couldn't be the Gods of the churches, it seems to me that you're something much bigger, something much greater than any of us can understand. And maybe *that's* the point. Maybe the point is to try and be the best person we can be, to love and be nice, so that we can be happy. I know *I'm* happiest when I'm having fun and playing nice with those around me," I nod, staring vacantly at the hustle and bustle of the parking lot and boat ramp.

"And, um, well," I gulp, wrapping my arms around myself. "I think there's something wrong with me. Well, *I* don't think it's wrong, but other people do. And I wish I could understand *why* you'd allow that to happen. I wish I could understand why you'd *want* that to happen. I wish I could see how that serves a purpose, but I can't.

"So, Gods, I ask that you please help me understand you. Help me understand faith. And please bring us rain, because it's very dry right now, and the lake is very low, and I don't like it. But please not too much rain, or then the lake will flood and that's a mess. Just enough rain to bring up the marina a few feet, please.

"And, Gods, I would also like to thank you. Thank you very much for Bucksaw and for my family." I say earnestly, loosening my arms and popping the sacred offering of bubblegum into my mouth.

THE FROG NO MORE

"Hey! Waste not, want not," I grin impishly at the sky.

*****

Wispy stratus clouds streak the afternoon sky, the shade of mammoth mossy oak trees beginning to creep over the shallow end of the pool. I stand waist-deep, one hand on my hip while the other twirls my shiny orange sunglasses. Mom stretches out on an ancient gold sun lounger, a book in one hand and a slender Marlboro Light in the other. Her hair is pulled up in a clippie and she wears large black sunglasses. She smiles at me as I splash about the pool, tossing my sunglasses near the stairs, and I am convinced she is the most beautiful woman in the world.

"What're you reading?" I chirp, tossing a ball toward the shimmering deep end of the pool.

"*The Runaway Jury* by John Grisham," she answers, bending her knees and resting the thick black hardcover against them.

"You and Grandpa John are *obsessed* with John Grisham," I tease. "Let me guess, he read it in a day and then gave it to you?"

"A day and a half," she smirks. "And it still wasn't quick enough!"

"I bet he laid on his long green couch and just read and read," I muse.

"Oh, I'm sure of it. I'm only forty pages in and already wrapped up!"

"What's your favorite book by John Grisham, Mom?" I ask, using my toe to trace the letters of Bucksaw Point Resort painted in red and yellow on the floor of the pool.

"Hmm," she sighs, laying her head on the sun lounger. "Probably *The Client*," she decides.

"What's it about?"

"It's about a wise young boy who helps a lawyer solve a murder case."

"Oh, wow! That sounds exciting! Do you think I would like his books?"

"One day. They're a bit much for you now, kinda like Anne Rice's vampires, but one day I suspect you'll really enjoy them," she nods.

"Hey! I'm making my way through *Interview with the Vampire* just fine!" I quip. "I mean, sometimes I get kinda confused, but for the most part I understand what's going on."

"I still can't believe I'm letting you read that book," she shakes her head with a smirk. "You're incorrigible."

"What does that mean?"

Mom inhales deeply, tips her head slightly to the left, and pulls the book closer to her chest.

"You're unapologetic with your interests, and I love your independence of thought! You've got an old soul. It means you're my wise little man, and it's sometimes hard for me to get in your way. I know it's my job, as a parent, to protect you and shield you from certain things until you're older, but you've got an awareness that other children don't often have. You're very perceptive—you understand people much better than your average ten-year-old."

"I dunno, Mom. Mason makes better grades than me, and so does Melissa. I don't think I'm dumb, but I don't think I'm very smart, either."

"Oh, honey, you're very smart. Of course, you are. But what I'm talking about has nothing to do with school or grades. What I mean is that you have a deep love and understanding of people, and you're able to see the big picture and empathize with adults in a way that most children can't. You're wise beyond your years, babe."

"Kinda like the kid in *The Client*?"

"Kinda," she agrees.

"Thank you, Mom. Sometimes I really don't feel very smart. Math always makes me feel like the dumbest boy in the world, and that makes me feel better, hearing you say all that. And I'm excited to read John Grisham when I get older. He's got to be good, the way you and Grandpa John tear through his books!"

"I'm so happy you love to read, Bub. It's such a gift to have a love for reading. It's the best way to escape to other places and worlds, to lose yourself in the story of someone else, to just have fun," she says wistfully. "Your Granny Doris taught me the joy of reading when I was a little girl, and I'm so happy to pass it on to you."

"Granny Doris has read more books than anyone I know!" I bellow, spinning circles.

"She sure has! What do you think is *your* favorite book?" Mom asks.

"Well, um, let me see," I ponder, diving under the water and sinking to the floor. I open my mouth and let out small air bubbles, considering my mom's question as they wriggle to the surface.

"*Beauty* by Bill Wallace," I shout, bursting from the pool's floor.

"Is that the sad one about the boy and his horse you had me read last year?"

"Yup, but it's only sad at the end. Everything else is actually really happy and fun. Well, not *everything* else, but you know what I mean!"

"Excellent choice," she beams. "Have you thought any more about reading *The Lord of The Rings*?"

"They're just *so long*, Mom! But I know you love them, so I'll give them a shot."

"Right on! Oh! We can even buy you a nice set of hardcovers!"

"Okay, cool! And *The Lion, the Witch and the Wardrobe*! Can we get that book, too?" I squeal with excitement.

"Sure, we can get that book, too. It's actually part of a series called *The Chronicles of Narnia*, and I read them all when I was younger. I was very into fantasy when I was your age, too."

"Hey, the vampire books are called chronicles, too. What does that word mean, Mom?"

"Oh, you're right! I'd never put that together, but you're right. A chronicle is a big, long story or historical event told in the order it happened. That's why some books are called chronicles."

"Cool, that makes sense! And I like adventure, too! Remember when you read *Treasure Island* to me and Dad? I loved that book!"

"Oh, I had forgotten all about that! Do you also remember the storm we drove through while I was reading that?" she gasps.

I tilt my head, then widen my eyes in recognition. "*Yes*! That was a *huge* storm, Mom! In all my years, I've never seen another one like it!"

"All your years, huh?" Mom repeats with a muffled giggle.

"Yeah! I remember Dad driving, and the clouds turning black, and then being stuck under a bridge or something for a long time while the storm passed."

"Yup," Mom nods. "It was a big overpass, and we were driving back to Missouri from Texas. I think we were almost to Oklahoma when that storm hit, in Granny Norma Jean's Cadillac. That was a fun trip, though."

"It really was! I remember I wasn't scared, because I was with you and Dad, and it was fun to read *Treasure Island* while it was storming. It made the book feel more real," I grin.

"It was exciting, wasn't it?" she fawns.

"Do you remember *another* exciting time in Granny Norma Jean's Cadillac?" I ask, twirling in the water.

"What's that?"

"Remember when we were driving home from visiting Granny Doris in Arkansas, and we slid on the ice into a ditch?" I say, attempting to suppress a cheesy grin.

"Oh, yes," she sighs. "But why are you smirking?"

"All I remember is being covered by *so many* blankets in the front seat, and then they all flew off me into the floorboard as you screamed out cuss words—and I'd never heard you say those words before and thought it was so darn funny! I mean, I'd heard you say 'shit' and 'damn it,' but I'd never heard you—" I clamp my hand to my mouth, stricken with panic. "I'm sorry, Mom! I don't know what came over me—I just cussed!"

Mom guffaws from the sun lounger, leaning on her side in stitches, and lets her book tumble to the ground.

"Oh, honey, it's okay! I know it was an honest mistake! And if I don't want you to say those words, I shouldn't say them around you," she giggles, wiping a tear from her eye.

"But they *are* kind of fun to say!" I acknowledge, realizing the delicious texture of cuss words on my tongue.

"Yes, well, let's not make a habit of it, alright?" she says with a stern yet cheeky wink, plucking her book from the ground and removing her bookmark.

"Sure thing, I promise! And happy reading!" I cry with joy, diving under the water for a one-person tea party and whispering the word shit three times.

THE FROG NO MORE

*****

Tying my reins around the saddle horn, I stretch my arms wide and place them behind me, relaxing on Jack's plump rump. We plod along the trail ride slowly but surely, ever the caboose, but happy, joyous, and free nonetheless. Fourteen other horses and mules trek ahead of us: my dad, on his fierce mule Comet, and Scott, riding his Palomino, Goldie, lead the way.

Sunlight breaks through the leaves above, creating scattered patches of shadows on the forest floor. I breathe deeply, relishing the scent of pine and wild honeysuckle. Plucking a twig from a passing elm tree, I rub it up and down Jack's neck, ruffling his mane.

"What a day, huh, Jack?" I giggle to myself, ducking to avoid a low-hanging branch.

"Does anyone have any soda?" Ed, my mom and dad's old high school friend, hollers from in front of me.

"I do, Ed!" I chirp. "I have Coke and Dr. Pepper."

"No Pepsi?" he groans.

"Nope, sorry—my mom might have a Pepsi in her saddlebag, though."

"Hey, Brenda!" Ed yells to my mom, who rides a few horses ahead of us.

"Yeah?" she answers, twisting backward in her saddle.

She is radiant, her black Ray-Ban's glinting in the sunlight magnificently. She wears high-waist Levi blue jeans and a white bikini top, her hair pulled into a ponytail with a white scrunchie.

"Got a Pepsi?" Ed leans forward hopefully.

"Are you drinking rum and Pepsi again, Ed?" Mom smiles. "You know that's absolutely disgusting!"

"Hey now, you don't know what you're talking about, woman! Now, do you have any Pepsi up there?"

"As a matter of fact, I do, but I don't think I should let you ruin it with rum," she quips, turning forward in her saddle.

"Damn it, Brenda!" Ed laughs. "Chuck, help me out here!"

"Oh, I know better than to get in between you two when you're fussing! You're on your own, bud," Dad grins, shrugging his shoulders.

"You're nasty, Ed!" Mom cackles, pulling a can of Pepsi from her saddlebag and handing it to Kathy, who rides behind her on a gorgeous chestnut mare named Katie. Kathy hands it to her daughter, Sarah, one of my best friends, bopping along on her paint horse Casey, who hands it back to Ed.

"Thank you, Sarah! Finally!" he sighs with satisfaction, cracking open his can of Pepsi, grabbing a bottle of rum from his saddlebag, and mixing them together in a cup.

"Care for a nip, Charlie?" Ed asks loudly, smirking.

"Ed, you little shit stain, don't you *dare*!" My mom shouts, turning to point her finger at Ed.

"Oh, c'mon, Brenda, just a nip—he might like it. *He* might have some class and taste," Ed guffaws.

"Just a nip, Mom, please!" I plead.

"Absolutely not!" Mom warns seriously, her nostrils flaring. "I mean it, Ed!"

"Fine, fine!" Ed holds his hands up in surrender, yet after Mom faces forward, he turns with a wink and discreetly passes his concoction to me.

I smile devilishly, catch a whiff of the cup's syrupy, pungent odor, and take a big gulp. Heat spreads down my throat and stomach, and I try my hardest not to cough. Swallowing, my eyes slightly watering, I tip the cup to my lips one more time, then hand it to Ed. He offers me a proud, smug grin.

"Not bad, eh?" he whispers.

"Not bad," I lie. "Kinda sweet," I tell the truth.

As we roam the hills of the forest and pristine valleys in between, I feel the effects of Ed's drink spilling over me. My feet are gloriously numb within their stirrups, and I have an overwhelming urge to scream cuss words or song lyrics at the top of my lungs. It is taking everything I have to hold in my current obsession, "Wannabe" by the Spice Girls.

Closing my eyes, I tip my head to the sky and the sun warms my face. Discovering numbness in my lips, too, I blow air through them, making fart noises and snickering. If this feeling happens from only a few sips of Pepsi and rum, I agree with Ed—my mom doesn't know *what* she's talking about! I swear the sun is brighter, and the trees are greener than before. My heart skips cheerfully in my chest, elation overtaking me.

THE FROG NO MORE

"Oh, Jack, I wish you liked to run!"

Dad and Scott bring us to the pasture with my favorite abandoned old house, made of moldering pale stones, the ceiling in shambles, and the once grand wooden porch sagging and weathered. I adore this forlorn pasture, with its decaying and decrepit house, and spend hours here with Granny Norma Jean and Brod, having picnics while watching clouds.

Hopping off Jack, I wrap his lead rope around a sturdy walnut tree, mindful to give him enough slack to graze and nibble, then scamper onto the creaking porch.

"Sarah! Come on, it's safe to go inside!" I call, prancing through the front door, which is merely two hinges covered by scraps of clinging wood. Sarah, born on Halloween and a fan of all things spooky, follows me inside, excited and grinning.

"I think this used to be the kitchen, see the rusted old stove?" I say, motioning to my left.

"And back there was probably the bedroom," she points to a roofless room with half the floor rotted away. "You're sure this is safe, Charlie?" she chortles. "Most of the roof is missing!"

"Oh yeah, Brod and I crawl around in here all the time. But you do have to step lightly and don't touch the walls. They crumble in some spots."

"Oh, wow," Sarah breathes. "But it *is* really cool. And probably so creepy at night!"

"You know, I've never been here at night, but I bet you're right! There are a few old tombstones in the back, under those trees out back," I guide her to an empty window frame, gesturing to several chipped and leaning tombstones.

"What? This is *amazing*! We've *got* to go look at those tombstones!" she exclaims with glee.

"Okay! There's only one that you can still read, and I think the person died in like 1880 or something, but I can't remember."

"C'mon, Charlie!" Sarah cries eagerly, bounding through a missing section of the back wall into the grassy yard behind the house.

I chase after her, shrieking with giggles and wishing the effects of Ed's drink could last forever.

BUCKSAW POINT RESORT & MARINA

*****

"Shit stains and early morning piss all over the sheets! Yeah, yeah, yeah! Oh shitty shit, we're going to the dam! Yeah, yeah, yeah! And a merry ol' bitch and piss and shit—yeah, yeah, yeah!" I sing to myself, relishing my newfound love of cuss words and giggling as I skip along the dock to Granny Norma Jean's pontoon.

It is late afternoon on the Fourth of July, and most of my family—Mom, Dad, Brod, Granny Norma Jean, Grandpa John, Uncle Chris and Aunt Dena, Aunt Trella and Uncle Tom, Granny Norma Jean's sister Aunt Judye and Uncle Bill with cousins Marnie and Amanda—will all cram ourselves onto Granny Norma Jean's pontoon and make our way to the dam. Each year on the Fourth of July, a massive fireworks show is held at the dam, and it is my first time witnessing the spectacle. Marnie and Amanda have each been once before, and both gushed profusely about the festivities.

Leaping from the dock to the front of Granny Norma Jean's pontoon, I wave at my mom as she battles the dock hose and cleans our gigantic white cooler on the back of the boat.

"Hi, Mom!" I chirp.

"Hey, babe," she says, her mouth pinched from the smell of the grimy cooler.

"You need some help?" I ask.

"I do, actually, yes," she answers, rinsing the cooler with the dock hose. "Would you mind busting up those bags of ice for me?"

"Sure!" I say happily. "Busting up ice bags is my favorite chore of them all."

"Thanks, babe. Just two or three for now, and then we'll pour more ice over after we've filled it with some sodas and beer."

"Gotcha," I say, hoisting a heavy bag of ice onto my shoulder and stepping onto the dock. Taking a deep breath, I lift the bag high above my head, then slam it down on the stone slabs of the dock.

"Are you excited, Mom? I'm so excited, I can hardly stand it!"

She wipes her brow with the back of her hand and smiles. "It's gonna be pretty cool."

"You and Dad went right after Bucksaw was built, right?"

"We sure did," Mom nods. "I think it was a year or two after Bucksaw opened, and it's quite the event! Lots of people drive their pontoons and boats and tie up together, like how we do in the coves, and we'll just eat and float and celebrate."

"Sounds magnificent!" I shudder with anticipation. "What time are we leaving? How long will it take us to get to the dam from here?"

"Oh, we'll probably leave here around eight, and it'll take us an hour and a half to get there," Mom answers, positioning the cooler under the pontoon's table on the floor of the boat, snug against the back seat.

"This is going to be so great!" I yelp. "Mom, can we make this a tradition? Can we do this *every* Fourth of July?" I lift another bag of ice, slamming it to the ground in merriment.

"Well, as long as you don't have any horse shows, I suppose this would make an excellent tradition for the Fourth of July, huh?"

"Yup!" I agree. "An excellent tradition! I love you, Mom! I love Bucksaw, I love our life!"

"Oh, buddy, I love you, too! I love our Bucksaw life, too!" she beams, stepping through the pontoon gate and scooping me into a hug.

Heaving the final bag into the air, I am filled with appreciation for the world around me. I wish to spend my life at Bucksaw, to take over the family business and spend my days running the resort. I want all of my family to live around the lake and help me run Bucksaw, and when Brod grows up, she can build a cozy cabin behind the pavilion. I want my family to live and work here, happy and busy, scurrying around Bucksaw forever. I want things to stay *exactly like this* forever.

Yes, that sounds quite perfect, indeed.

3

Antioch

Summer/Fall 1999
Clinton, Missouri
13 Years Old

Aimlessly wandering our unfinished basement, I lightly graze my fingertips across the prickly and coarse concrete walls. The house is silent and still. Empty. Is that how I feel? Empty? Or am I in shock? Am I blindsided and gobsmacked? Am I dumbfounded with heartache in this drab basement?

I'm aware. I understand Mom died from a massive stroke brought on by an aneurysm. I remember watching her convulse and foam at the mouth. I remember the hospital, the funeral, and all of my family and friends swarming around Dad, Brod, and me. I remember it *all*, vividly, but none of it seems *real*. It's as if I'm navigating an infinite, tormenting nightmare.

No, I'm not sure what I feel, but I don't think it's emptiness. There's too much swirling within my chest and my mind. Anger, yes, although less than before, less than the moments immediately following Mom's passing. Sadness, definitely, but that's to be expected and natural. No, there's something else overriding it all, something elusive and dominant; something lurking and prodding.

Heartbreak, perhaps, for me and Brod. Heartbreak for Brod, six years old and without a mother. She barely got any time with Mom, it doesn't seem

THE FROG NO MORE

fair. It doesn't seem right. Motherless. Cheated. How will Brod grow up without a mom? And what will I do? Who will I talk to? How will I ever be able to be myself without her support? How can I "come out" without her by my side? What will my poor dad do? How will he manage without my mom's help?

We are lost, the lot of us. Lost and broken and forsaken.

Drifting toward the sliding glass door, I stare vacantly at our backyard: long and wide, with manicured green grass until the tree line. I hate it. I hate this house. I hate living on land, in town. I hate having neighbors. I hate the noise of traffic. I hate that there's no privacy. I hate that my mom died and the world didn't explode for everyone else. I hate that I don't know what to feel. Or what to do. I hate and I hate and I hate! But it is just *another* feeling, it is not *the* feeling. The big one. The one I don't understand, the one that truly frightens me. What *is* it? Why does it take my breath away? Why does it give me goosebumps?

Granny Norma Jean, Aunt Trella, and Aunt Dena will feed us, do the laundry, and clean the house. I should help, though. I shouldn't let them do everything. Mom was Trella's sister, her best friend, and my heart hurts for her, too. Mom and Trella were always together, working or having fun, what will Trella do now? How will she cope, after losing not only her best friend but her sister, too? I shiver, a dense lump burning in my throat.

No! I don't want to cry anymore. My eyes hurt from crying and it doesn't seem to do much good. I've wailed, sobbed, poured buckets, and silently quivered, all to no avail. My evasive emotional storm remains beyond my grasp. And Brod doesn't need to see me falling apart, she doesn't need to see me sulking around, she needs guidance and love.

Gently tapping the glass of the sliding door, I spin on the ball of my foot and ascend the staircase to the main floor. There's no reason for me to hate this house, for it's quite beautiful. Mom was adamant about an open-design floor plan and selected a dashing home. Each room has lofty tray ceilings, and the magnificently grand kitchen, with its sleek white countertops and marvelous fanciful cabinets, can be seen from any room in the house. The kitchen flows elegantly into a spacious living room, boasting a flashy fireplace framed by floor-to-ceiling windows with views of the backyard. I tread across the polished hardwood floors into the dining room, where a bay window overlooks the front yard, containing a lone sapling in a berm, the carport, and a winding path to the front door, speckled by bushes spaced evenly before a slender concrete stoop.

Suburbia, but *not* the country, even if it is on the outskirts of town.

However, I have to admit, it *is* a very beautiful house. But I still hate it. Mom suffered her first seizure here, then died in the hospital. When we bought this house, my mom was alive, but now, she's gone. And this stupid house goes on standing! I hate it and wish it were gone, burned to the ground, and my mom was alive. I want to blame this house for my mom's death, but I know that doesn't make sense. I want to hurt this house because I was hurt while living in it, and I also know that doesn't make sense. But it's how I *feel*.

My head turns to her senior portrait hanging on the dining room wall. She smiles demurely. Her eyes are big and blue, just like Brod's. The same color as mine. I see myself in her face. I have her bone structure and touch the frame reverently. Would Mom know what I'm feeling? Would she know what to tell me? Probably. But she's not here to do that anymore, ever again. I'll have to get used to that, won't I?

I catch the reflection of our entertainment center in the glass of her portrait and bow my head. Should I play some of her favorite music? Maybe Fleetwood Mac, Counting Crows, or Matchbox Twenty? Or maybe I should play *my* favorite of her favorites, Tracy Chapman? Yes, that's the one, some Tracy! Crossing from the dining room to the living room through a faux hallway made of pillars, I swing open the door to the CD player of the entertainment center and scan the drawer holding my mom's collection of CDs. Selecting Tracy's debut album, *Tracy Chapman*, I crank up the volume and flop onto our plush hunter-green leather couch.

This should be any teenager's dream: complete freedom in a gigantic suburban house equipped with every modern fixture known to man. A fridge full of food, cabinets stocked with every conceivable snack, and a comfortable bedroom with an expensive stereo system and mounted TV. I'd give it *all* up in a *heartbeat* to have my mom back. I'd gladly live on an island with nothing if it meant my family could be whole again. If it meant my heart could be whole again.

"Talkin' 'bout a Revolution" blares from the speakers and I curl into a ball, focusing on the sunlight spilling upon our wooden and etched glass coffee table, casting rainbows on the off-white Berber carpet. It is the ornate coffee table from the hotel lobby of Bucksaw, and I am stabbed by a pang of nostalgia.

As "Fast Car" begins, I rise from the couch and step into the kitchen. Brazenly, I open the liquor cabinet above the snack drawer. My eyes linger over the sparkling bottles, coming to a rest on an amber-colored bottle of Southern Comfort. Comfort sounds nice, comfort sounds good. But what should I drink with Southern Comfort? Coke? I shrug, grabbing the handle of the bottle, and the liquor swirls inside, making a tinkling noise. Placing the Southern Comfort on our island, I take a Coke from the fridge and choose a tall glass from the cabinet. How much liquor should I pour? A third of Southern Comfort? Half? Half of the glass sounds good. Nodding to myself, I pour the Coke over the Southern Comfort and bring the glass to my nose. Fizzy bubbles tickle my nostrils, emitting a sweet, biting scent.

I falter, conflicted, and set the glass on the island. The last time I got drunk, I ended up feeling guilty and ashamed. Left alone at Granny Norma Jean's house in the country, I raided the outdoor fridge on her back porch and guzzled five beers. While the beer *did* provide a delightful sense of escapism, I've never burped and peed more in my life and was ultimately met with the crushing force of reality and a dull headache a few hours later. And what would my mom say about all this sudden drinking of mine?

It dawns on me: escapism. *That* is the feeling! The yearning for an escape from the pain of my life. I want the life of my boyhood, traipsing around Bucksaw without a care in the world. What would I say to that boy? Would I tell him his life would flip upside down as soon as he became a teenager? That everything he knew and loved would be ripped from him two weeks after his thirteenth birthday? Would it have made it easier, knowing my mom was going to die? Probably not. Probably the way it happened was for the best, swift and clean, like the slice of a knife to my heart.

No, I shouldn't drink this Southern Comfort and Coke. This isn't right, my mom wouldn't want me to do this. Plucking the glass from the island, I dump its contents down the sink and rinse everything with hot water. Steam rises and I lift my gaze to the window as a crimson-feathered cardinal soars across our backyard.

"Mom?" I breathe, my heart thundering in my chest.

Tracy continues to croon as I meander through the kitchen and living room, hugging myself. Should I lay on the floor and sing Tracy Chapman? Would that give me a feeling of escapism? Should I read *Harry Potter* fan fiction until the wee hours of the morning, eating pickles and vinegar while I become lost in my own private world? Should I run away and join the circus? Should I call myself "The World's Most Emotional and Dramatic Boy" and glare daggers from the cage of a carnival?

"No, you're talking madness again," I mutter, finding myself at the staircase to the basement.

Harry Potter fan fiction it is, then. I clap my hands loudly, creating echoes, decide to let Tracy finish her album, and descend the carpeted staircase to my lair of angst.

*****

"You found *weed*?" I repeat ecstatically, pressing the phone tightly against my ear as Penelope explains how she happened upon a joint for us to smoke. "Okay, I'll see you soon to do drugs!"

I place my cordless phone back on its charger and spring from the bed, elation blooming within me. Tonight I will smoke marijuana for the first time in my life! The desire to try it has grown over the last few weeks and I'm ready for a new intoxicant. I'm ready to experiment beyond drinking, to lean toward my devious side, to be a *little hellion*! I'm ready to blot out the monotony of this everyday, sour, mundane life.

Penelope lives less than a quarter of a mile away, and I anxiously await her arrival. Pacing the floors of our house, I sip water and reapply deodorant, the anticipation of smoking weed making me sweat more than usual. There is a rush of adrenaline in knowing I'm behaving recklessly. It's satisfying to be bad. It feels good.

Our doorbell rings and I gallop from the kitchen to unlock the front door, delinquency surging through my veins.

"Hey," Penelope says, closing the front door behind her, an impish glint in her hazel eyes. "You ready to get stoney bologna?"

"Yup! Here, follow me," I wave to the back deck door and lead us to the side of the house facing the tree line, where we will be shielded from any unwelcome snooping.

"Are you excited?" Penelope grins, taking a black lighter and the joint from her pocket. It is wrapped in white rolling paper, long and slim.

"I'm *so* freaking excited! And I have lots of snacks in case we get hungry!"

"Perfect," she says, flicking the lighter and inhaling smoke. She holds her breath for several seconds, then coughs loudly and fiercely, handing me the joint.

"Are you okay?" I ask.

"Yeah, coughing is a *good* thing," she giggles.

I bring the joint to my lips and take a drag as though I were smoking a cigarette. Smoke fills my lungs, hot and thick, and I hold it in for as long as possible, then double over in a fit of violent coughs. I pass the joint to Penelope and straighten my back.

"Whoa, that kind of hurt—I coughed so hard it felt like I pulled a muscle in my butthole! But it also tasted kind of good, almost like scrambled eggs."

Penelope bursts into laughter, smoke expelling from her mouth forcefully, and I pinch the joint from her fingers.

"I don't feel anything yet, I'm going to take two hits in a row," I decide, inhaling deeply.

"Damn, don't Bogart that shit!" she groans playfully.

"What in the hell does that mean?" I ask, realizing smaller hits don't make me cough as much.

"It means you're hogging the joint, now pass it over!"

"My bad," I shrug, offering her the joint.

"You're not feeling anything *at all*?"

"I dunno. Maybe it's too soon to tell. It usually takes me a few minutes after a shot of booze, maybe this is the same way?"

"Well, *I'm* starting to feel it, and I feel fucking *great!*" she beams, and indeed her eyes have turned rather glassy.

We pass the joint back and forth, coughing and giggling, until it is too tiny to handle, and then bury it in the grass beside the house. I lean against the garage door and gaze over the fields around our house.

"Uh-oh," I say, "someone's cow got out."

"What?" Penelope chortles, squatting on the ground to my left.

"Someone's cow—look," I point to the next lot over. "It got out somehow."

"Oh, my God, Charlie! You're high as a kite!" Penelope squeals with laughter, falling onto her side.

"What?" I ask, confused by her response.

"That's a grill with a cover on it next to a bush!" she shrieks, tears streaming down her cheeks. "Oh, that's so funny! You thought it was a cow!"

"Damn, I *am* stoned! But can't you see how I thought that was a cow?" I titter. "Oh, yeah, I definitely feel it now! This is amazing, Penelope! Oh, why haven't we been doing this the whole time?"

*****

Slouched against the metal pole of the sign for our drive, Antioch, I flick my cigarette toward the center of the street. Red sparks scatter over the pavement, the embers smoldering into a wisp of smoke. It is nearing three in the morning and my urge to be destructive, devious, and devilish is at an all-time high. Over these last few weeks, my anger has grown to a boiling rage and it is beginning to become overwhelming. I wonder how much longer it will be before I'm unable to contain its wraith.

The streetlamps create garish halos in the early morning fog, and as I pass beneath each one, I envision shredding them to bits with the power of telekinesis. I imagine destroying every cookie-cutter house in my neighborhood, impaling the sleek, expensive vehicles parked in the driveways, and setting fire to the fields and open lots, causing the ground to quake, crack, and spew magma. In my mind's eye, I am the harbinger of chaos and desolation.

"I am the God of Wreckage," I mutter, a bitter smile twitching on my lips.

Darkness is soothing, darkness is calming. Darkness is constant and will never abandon me. I have found my salvation in darkness, wandering the woods at night like a vampire. I wish to build a castle with no windows so that I can stalk from room to room and never witness the sun, listen to dreary classical music, sip fine red wine, eat Xanax, and chain-smoke Marlboro Light cigarettes.

Lately, I *prefer* anger over any other emotion. Anger is easier to understand. It's easier to manipulate and sustain. Anger patiently simmers under the surface, waiting to rise and conquer whatever needs to be conquered. I am enamored with anger, and thoroughly enjoy basking in the high and purpose it provides. My anger is stronger than my sadness, and I am grateful for its power to obliterate.

Clenching my fists at my sides, I walk behind our house and sit underneath our stilted back porch, making it a point to sit in the exact spot I sat in moments after Mom's fatal seizure, and light another cigarette. One more cigarette and then I'll go back inside, wash my hands, brush my teeth, spray cologne, and crawl under the sheets, where I will stare at the ceiling for another few hours until the sun rises yet again. On rare nights, I am able to sleep four or five hours, but most of the time, I linger somewhere between sleeping and waking.

"I need to go to the bookstore so I can keep myself occupied on these long nights," I murmur, craning up at the stars. "What should I buy, Mom? The new Nicholas Sparks book sounds good. I can't remember what it's called—something about a walk, I think. Or should I pick up the last book you were to ever read by John Grisham, *The Testament*? I can see its cover when I close my eyes, and it makes me think of you."

A blackbird sings and I snuff my cigarette. Trudging to the furthest tip of our backyard, before the tree line, I kick up a bit of dirt with my tennis shoe and bury my cigarette butt. There's no sense in getting caught by my dad, and I am painstakingly careful to hide my smoking from him. Although, maybe I should stop burying them? That can't be good for the environment. I swear,

I can't win for losing.

Slipping through the sliding glass door of the basement, I slink up the stairs to my bathroom, wash up, spritz myself, and tip-toe to my room. Curling under my sheets, I peer at the field across the street through my tall, thin windows. An early commuter idles by, setting off an idea in my mind: what if I actually *did* run away in the dead of night? What if I simply ran away from all the pain, anger, and frustration of my life? What if I removed myself from the depravity of Clinton, Missouri and sought refuge in a thriving capital of culture and acceptance? What if I ran away to Chicago or New York City? Or maybe even Los Angeles or Miami?

How do I run away, though? Are there really still circuses to join? I suppose if I put my mind and body into it, anything is possible. And if anything is possible, that means it's also possible for me to find happiness and meaning right where I'm at. If *anything* is possible, that means I truly *am* in control, whether I want to admit it or not. And I'd rather not admit it. I'd rather lean toward the grim despair of a gloomy life in which I need to constantly and continuously run. A life where I never settle, where I never stay still long enough for my emotional baggage to catch up with me.

A life of avoidance.

But it would be yet another shocking blow to my dad and sister. It would not be fair to them and would not give my life the merit I seek. No, I must work with the situation at hand.

"Work with what you've got," I whisper. "Be thankful for what you've got. Stop wallowing, stop bitching, stop whining. You're not the first gay boy to lose his mom. You're not the only one in this world suffering. Pick yourself up and *live*! Push all your anger and sadness to the side, and *do* something with your life. Make Mom proud."

A hot tear slides over my nose and down my cheek, dropping to the pillow with a faint thud. The sound of flowing air whirls from the air conditioner vent and I roll onto my back, spreading my arms wide.

"I don't *mean* to be a selfish, forlorn boy. I don't mean to seem bratty. I know I am privileged in many ways—that is not lost on me. But I can't help the way I *feel*, you know? I don't know. Just please help me. Is there anyone out there listening? Gods? Guardians of the East? Mom? Please help this confused, angry, and depressed gay boy. Please help me. Please."

*****

Gripping the edge of the sink with my left hand and the countertop of the island with my right, I launch my legs into the air and swing back and forth, belting Sarah McLachlan's "Building a Mystery" at the top of my lungs. Dad is fetching Brod from dance and I have busied myself preparing our dinner to the ballads of Sarah. Noodles simmer on the stove and the oven is on pre-heat for four hundred degrees. We shall dine on chicken and noodle casserole tonight, and I desperately hope it's better than my previous attempts at cooking dinner.

Dad and Brod are patient with me, and since I've grown proficient at making tacos, I reckon a casserole shouldn't be *too* difficult. Cooking is proving to be an excellent distraction, as well, and far superior to the brooding anger that gripped me for weeks. Shedding my skin of rage, and ceasing to drink alcohol or smoke weed, I have embraced cooking, cleaning, and reading with great vigor. Avoiding my emotional debacle by keeping busy, I am infinitely more pleasant now that my sadness and anger have been replaced. By discovering routines that aid in banishing my overpowering and oppressive emotions, my daily life has become much more tolerable.

Cher, our black and tan dachshund puppy, yaps down the hallway and barrels around the corner of the kitchen, her tiny toenails clicking on the hardwood floor.

"Hi, baby girl!" I coo as she sniffs and licks my ankles. "Come here."

Cradling her tenderly in my arms as if she were a newborn baby, which in a way I suppose she is, I croon the lyrics of "Sweet Surrender" and sway side to side. Our kitchen is aglow with the soft lighting of the cabinets, and I embrace this moment of profound peace. Cher locks eyes with me and I kiss her long snout.

"You're the sweetest little thing that there ever was!" I fawn, planting dozens of kisses on her head. "And I wish you'd sleep with me at least *one* night a week! But you're Brod's girl, and I get it. And that's good, that's perfect. You know, Brod sure does need you right now, Cherbear," I sigh, placing her gently on the floor and turning to the stove.

The garage door opens, rumbling and creaking, and I tip my head to the side, wearing a poignant grin. Mom may have died, and our family may have been irrevocably broken, but we will persevere. We will bind together and make it through this devastating series of events. We will lean on one another, and we will be okay.

"Yeah, Mom," I whisper lovingly, "we're gonna be okay."

4

Loss of Innocence

Fall 2001
Bethlehem Township (Clinton), Missouri
15 Years Old

This land is ancient, hallowed, and quiet. It is to be observed and respected, miraculously untouched by human expansion over the years, and I think it is perfect. The perfect place to drive my four-wheeler, the perfect place to lose myself, safe in the middle of a meadow, surrounded by towering trees that were centuries old before I was born. These rolling meadows, overgrown with sprouting wildflowers, and patches of oaks, walnuts, and silver maples, are sacred; they are a refuge where I can rest and recharge. I am a proud Son of the Forests.

Folding my arms behind my head and propping my feet on top of the handlebars of my red Kawasaki four-wheeler, I chuckle peacefully. The sky is pale blue and streaked with wisps of stratus clouds. Or are they altostratus clouds? I'm not sure. Did I learn that in the Third Grade? I have no idea, but they *are* pretty. Soothing, like a brush stroke of white paint on an endless blue canvas. The air is mild, warmer than usual for October, yet crisp, indicative of Missouri's delicate autumns.

I spot a hawk soaring above, circling for prey. Oh, to be able to fly! To have the power of traveling wherever I want, whenever I want.

Power.

That is my obsession, but not in the traditional sense. I do not have the desire to govern or become an elected official. The horrific attack on the World Trade Center solidified my aversion to political aspirations. It left me feeling small and alone. No, that is not the power I seek. I merely want the power to live a fantastic, artistic, and meaningful life. I want my time spent on Earth to matter. It's not that I want to be Harry Potter, although I would settle for Neville Longbottom. Hmm, a fan fiction where Neville travels all over the world, breaking hexes and curses and rescuing lost magical artifacts? That could be interesting!

I sigh. Should I start writing stories other than *Harry Potter* fan fiction? How else do I plan on obtaining an artistic life, if not through my words, my stories? But *what* do I write about? If Mom were here, she'd be able to give me an idea. She'd be able to inspire me.

Ah, Mom.

"I miss you," I whisper faintly to the wind. "Dad's married now, but then I'm sure you know that already. And it's weird. It's so weird and feels kind of wrong. But what else can I do, other than go with it and try to make the best of it? Brod seems happy enough, I guess. We're okay, I guess. But I do have a loyalty to you, and feel like I shouldn't approve of this marriage or something. I don't fuss, though, because I'm sure you'd tell me there's no need to hurt Dad by being a sullen brat."

Swallowing a lump in my throat, I rise, hastily start the four-wheeler, and rip across the meadow. Tree limbs whip by as I try to outrun my grief, as I try to pretend I'm okay. The snap of the tires crushing fallen tree limbs and the growl of the motor is a welcome soundtrack, blotting out all other sounds.

Focus. Faster. Blaze your four-wheeler across one meadow and into a thicket of trees. Watch out! Duck your head just in time to miss being decapitated. Faster! Press your thumb on the gas as hard as you can, and lean into the turns. The light of the meadow and the shadows of the forest blur together, their scents damp and sweet. *Faster*! Barrel over the pasture in a frenzy!

I burst into the pasture and come to an abrupt stop, out of breath and exhilarated. That was dangerous and foolish, but all-consuming and thrilling. What if something awful had happened, though? What would that do to my family? How selfish of me! How thoughtless!

"Ugh! Why is everything *such a fucking challenge?*" I scream to the sky, and my voice is raw, ragged with anguish.

I want to rage. I want to yell and holler and burn these fields to the ground! I want everyone in the world to know my pain, my anger. And I want a hug. I want to be held so tightly I can no longer breathe! I want to plant oak and walnut trees for the ones I destroyed. I want to love and embrace peace just as fiercely as I want to wallow in hate and destruction. I'm *all over* the damn place! Is it because I'm a Gemini? Is it because my mom died? Is it because I'm gay?

"It's because I'm human," I mutter thoughtfully.

Gay.

The word knocks around my head. I'm gay. Mom would have been able to help with that, too. I would have been able to tell her, to actually come out. Oh, why didn't I tell her before she died? I've known I'm gay since I was nine years old, but it didn't seem important to tell her yet. And would she like Colin, my online boyfriend? My fellow Potterhead? Would she think he is cute and funny like I do? Surely she would.

"You could have read my *Harry Potter* fan fiction and met my online boyfriend, and you would have loved them both," I say dismally. "I wish I could tell Dad. I wish I could share with Dad what I want to share with you. But I'm afraid it would be too much for him to handle right now. I'm afraid I'll disappoint him."

Does my dad already know I'm gay? Did he figure it out last year when he asked about my internet search history? And why did I lie? Why am I scared to tell my dad I'm gay? It's not like he's going to be mad or kick me out of the house. He's not like that. But what if he's sad? What if he suddenly doesn't understand me and pushes me away? I can't lose my dad, too. No, I can't tell my dad I'm gay, things are better the way they are. Besides, no one else in school is gay, so I should stay silent.

If I had power, none of these things would matter. If I had power, I could be whoever I want to be. If I wasn't a sad gay boy stuck in the country, I could do so many wonderful things.

"Ew, but don't feel sorry for yourself like a little brat bitch," I spat, shaking my head. "Get a grip!"

A breeze rustles the tall grass, carrying the faint aroma of flowers, and the sun breaks through the clouds, bright and glorious. Mom is warning me, telling me to calm down, to take it easy, and to remember she is always with me, no matter what.

"You're right, Mom. You're right," I murmur. "But I still miss you so damn much."

Starting the four-wheeler again, I make a wide circle in the pasture and decide to drive home carefully, enjoying the wind on my face and the sun on my back.

*****

Sprawled on my bed watching the ceiling fan spin lazily, I hear my computer ding, which can only mean one thing: Colin has messaged me! I spring from the bed and jump into my squishy office chair, scooting the mouse to awaken the monitor. The screen blinks to life and I click on his flashing icon.

>**Colin**: How was your day?

I drum my fingers on the keyboard, thinking.

>**Charlie**: Usual. I had PE today and we played volleyball, so it wasn't too terrible. I thought about you a lot today, and that made me happy, which made my day easier.

I lean back in my chair, anxiously awaiting his reply. I met Colin three months ago through my friend Jana, known online as "George Weasley's Girlfriend," after the two of them co-wrote a George Weasley fan fiction, which I read and adored. I emailed Jana, fawning over their masterpiece, who then emailed

Colin to share my praise. Shortly after, he and I began chatting, and within a few days, a relationship developed. They're part of my online *Harry Potter* world and the only thing that's kept me afloat lately. Colin and I have been dating for a little over two months, and even though we've never seen one another in person, I do believe I'm in love. My computer dings again.

> **Colin**: *blushes* I think about you all day, too. I go to Our Gay Common Room when I can't take school anymore.

Colin is referring to a magical fantasy mansion we've created with our imaginations, specifically a living room with a river running through the middle. It is there where we are able to secretly cuddle and kiss one another, among other things. Listen, cybersex isn't *that* bad, especially with someone as articulate as Colin.

> **Charlie**: Oh! I'm sorry I wasn't there to snuggle and snog you! *kisses*

The sun sets on the horizon outside of my bedroom window, purple and milky gold.

> **Colin**: It's okay. I cleaned and put my feet in the river. And thought about holding your hand IRL.

I pull my gaze from the setting sun and groan. Oh, Colin, if only! My fingers flash across the keyboard.

> **Charlie**: I wish I could tell my dad about you, and buy a plane ticket to visit you. Why does being gay have to be such a big deal to everyone? Why can't people be excited for us the same way they're excited for straight teenagers falling in love? It just seems so unfair, but I guess that's life.
>
> **Colin**: Right? And maybe one day we'll be at a place where gay boys

are being celebrated, but who knows? I so wish you could fly here, too! But I'd also probably fall over dead from panic because what if my parents found out about us?! And then you'd have to keel over right beside me, Romeo and Romeo style.

A smile twitches on my lips. I have a boyfriend, and no one in my "real life" knows. Honestly, I much prefer my online life to my real life; if only I had the unlimited financial freedom to build myself an oasis where I could live with my online friends. But, would it be as much fun if it were no longer a secret? Something tells me it wouldn't.

Colin: Hey, babe, unfortunately—GTG—my mom and dad just got home and need help unloading the van. Ugh. *kisses*
Charlie: Bye, babe! Chat later tonight? *kisses*
Colin: You bet!

A blue message advises Colin has logged out. I spin my chair in a circle, watching the windows of my room slowly glide by, then swipe my copy of *Blood and Gold* by Anne Rice from my nightstand.

"Ah, Marius, but *when* will the gay sex start?" I chuckle, cracking open my copy and resting on my messy bed.

Blood and Gold is the first Anne Rice book I've read since attempting to read *Interview with the Vampire* as a kid, although I've watched the movie version of *Interview with the Vampire* more times than I can count. Her depiction of vampires speaks to me. Their struggles and inner monologues move and stir my soul. To me, vampires are a great metaphor for being gay, for being an outsider desperately wanting acceptance and approval. I understand their plight of confining a part of themselves from the world, out of fear and self-preservation.

Being gay is the main reason I empathize with being an outsider. On the surface, I am a typical blond-haired, blue-eyed white boy from a relatively affluent family. I am an average Midwestern American carrying a secret. But this secret represents a great part of me, not necessarily because of my sexual preferences, but because of the gift it has given me: the capacity to love and accept, regardless of race, gender, or sexual identity. Division among ourselves, separating ourselves from others out of fear, and clinging to the idea of "keeping with one's own, keeping things as they are and always have been," are ideas that make absolutely no sense *whatsoever* to me. Why should I care about one's skin color, gender, religion, or choice of identity? Aren't we *all human beings* on this floating rock? Why must we divide ourselves based on such insubstantial attributes? Why are we perpetuating a culture of reacting with fear and disdain instead of curiosity and celebration?

"Oh, why couldn't I have been born in New York City, or somewhere like that? Where there's more acceptance and understanding!" I bemoan. "Ah, but would it have even mattered? Hate is everywhere, Charlie. Hate is *everywhere*," I remind myself.

Shaking my head to clear my thoughts, I remove my bookmark and allow Anne Rice to whisk me away to her dark, glamorous world of vampires and doomed love. Between witches, wizards, and vampires, I am emerging from my grief. I feel connected to my mom when escaping into the land of books, a favorite land of hers, a treasured land. And I'm sure it brings her great joy, watching me safe and sound as I escape to the land she first showed me.

*****

A full moon shines palely in the midnight blue sky, illuminating the darkness of the meadow. The silhouette of the forest is motionless, stars twinkling above its treetops. It is eerily quiet as I peer around, slide off my backpack, and pull out a large patchwork quilt sewn by my Granny Doris. Spreading it over the lush grass, I carefully arrange candles of different colors, shapes, and sizes in a circle. Taking a deep breath, I smirk and light their wicks, a faint breeze stirring the flames. Satisfied with my arrangement and confident they will remain lit, I sit crisscross, mindful to face the East.

"Oh, Charlie, people would think you're nuts if they could see you!" I sigh. "But whatever. At least I'm not dancing naked under the full moon. Although that *does* sound very fun."

Resting my hands on my knees, I close my eyes and focus on my surroundings, on the symphony of the night. The air is crisp and cool, crackling with early fall. An owl hoot resounds over the meadow, and I bow my head, steeling myself. This is not silly, this is not lame. This is an earnest boy asking for help during a very troubling time. Inhaling slowly through my nose, I open my eyes and stare at the night sky.

"I call upon the Watchtower of the East and beseech the Guardians of Air, Gemini, and Mercury. I summon you for the protection of this space and I summon you for guidance," I declare, surprised by the deep commanding tone of my voice. "And I'm sorry I'm not doing this properly and apologize for my ignorance. I simply wish to call upon the Watchtower of the East and ask the Guardians of Air, Gemini, and Mercury for help because I'm at my wit's end and have no spiritual guidance in my life. I'm not asking for magic—I'm asking for help. I'm asking to be seen and heard. *Please* accept my summoning!" I finish, my arms raised.

Silence rings, occasionally pierced by the tweet of a cricket or the screech of a cicada. Swallowing a tight lump of heat in my throat, I clench my fists and fight back tears. I'm an idiot! This is utterly foolish. The Watchtower of the East is a story and nothing more, stupid dumbass!

"But I don't *really* believe that!" I scream to the night. "I don't! Which is why I call upon the Watchtower of the East and the Guardians of Air, Gemini, and Mercury!"

Grief seizes me and I arch forward, sobbing. As tears stream down my cheeks, a tingly sensation begins to spill over my shoulders and arms, as though a warm fuzzy blanket has been placed around me. The wind whirls through the tree leaves—faintly, yes—but stronger than before. I raise my head, my tears weakening, and watch as the branches break free of their silhouette to sway against the starry sky.

"I feel you," I breathe, a smile blooming on my lips. "Mom?"

Standing hurriedly, I throw my arms open wide again.

"Thank you for listening to me! And please stay with me for a while! I need to get a few things off my chest, and ask a couple of questions."

I turn in each direction, breathless, the tingly sensation in my shoulders and arms spreading to my chest. Bringing my hands to my head, I look to the sky and grin. The wind fades, and while it was most likely nothing more than an average nighttime breeze, I revel in the thought of communing with a force greater than myself. And surely Mom has swooped in to catch the latest of my shenanigans?

"Okay, let me get my wits about me! Wow, this is exciting, but I'm so alone and confused, at least that's how I feel lately, and it's eating me up inside. Please help me figure out how to be true to myself. I don't feel like I'm living in a way that is true to who I am, and I need help with—."

I chew my top lip, flustered.

"What I mean is: what should I do? I feel fake right now. I don't feel like I'm listening to my soul. I'm pretending to be someone I'm not. I'm pretending to be flashy and snarky and cynical. I'm pretending to care about things that I don't actually care about.

"I *know* who I am, I *know* what's really important to me, but that boy—the one I used to be—well, I can't find him anymore. It's like he's a phantom, a memory. And I don't know how to look for him—I don't know how to find him. Does that make any sense? Oh, but surely you know what I mean! Because I don't want to go on this way anymore! I don't want to hide who I am, or live my life worried about other people's views and opinions! I don't want to live my life in fear and regret, because that's no way to live it all," I lament.

My eyes scan the stars and I focus on the Big Dipper, trying to collect my scattered and chaotic thoughts, emotions rippling throughout me.

"I want to be true to myself, and for my life to have meaning and purpose. I want that more than anything! I want to be who I *am*, and proud of that, so others can see it's okay to be different. We don't have to be repulsed and scared of people or ways of life we don't understand. I want other boys to know it's okay to be nerdy and obsessed with a fantasy world that isn't real. It's okay if it brings you joy! Being manly is not the 'end all, be all' of masculinity! Brains are just as important as brawn! We should be allowed to be ourselves, without having to worry about these stupid standards from the '50s, which was actually a shitty time for most people! Fucking *don't* leave it to dumbass Beaver—he got it all wrong! And I hate being afraid. I hate feeling like I can't be myself!" I spat.

"Oh, Guardians of the East, please help me be less angry. Please help me find enlightenment and peace in my path. I don't know why, but I have a nagging suspicion that my life isn't going to be easy, and it will all be self-inflicted out of fear and shame. I'm ruining myself by being fake. I'm ruining myself by pretending everything is okay, and sooner or later it will catch up with me."

A gust of wind extinguishes several candles and I freeze, surveying the area cautiously. The night remains still and I teeter on the tips of my toes, understanding it as a message.

"I'm onto something there, eh? Do you agree? Mom, if you're here, I know you'd want me to stay true to myself, to honor the person that I am. And you'd probably tell me to learn from all that has happened so I will be able to weather any storm. You'd tell me life is going to be rough, certainly, but it's also going to be beautiful and needs to be cherished.

"But I just don't know where that carefree, curious, and happy boy of my childhood went. It's like he died with you. The day you died, he died, too. My loss of innocence. Is that what it's called? When your world comes crashing down around you, and everything you knew is swept away in a matter of seconds? A part of me is empty without him—without you—and I don't know how to fill that part back up.

"I just want to be wild and free again, but I feel trapped. And everyone seems to like snarky, bitter Charlie—they think he's funny and witty. Which is a lot better than being called 'Charlie *Gay.*' It's *a lot* better than always being afraid I'm only moments away from getting my ass kicked. I don't really know what changed, but one day they decided I was funny, and I realized it was because I was being dark and macabre and sarcastic. I was actually mocking one of them in a moment of rare, brave stupidity, but they didn't realize it and laughed. It was nuts, Mom! It was like someone snapped their fingers and suddenly I was okay, suddenly I was accepted. I wasn't the weird gay guy from Leesville anymore. And now I'm just stuck with this—this—this *persona*, I guess. I don't know, I should probably consider myself lucky and quit bitching. But somehow, that doesn't seem fair to me."

Swaying gently, I fold my arms behind my back and close my eyes, grateful for the solitude of a quiet country night. I envision my spirit lifting from my body and taking flight toward the night sky. In my mind's eye, I fly across the meadows and ponds, exhilarated and emitting a benevolent gray and cobalt glow. Streaking across the stars, I chuckle fondly at my earthbound body before resuming my proper place and opening my eyes with a sigh.

"Guardians of the East, Air, Gemini, and Mercury, thank you for visiting with me. And please watch out for me, okay? Please make sure my life doesn't get too fucked up. And Mom, thanks for the tingly feeling, and thanks for taking care of me. I am so thankful for all of you, and cannot wait until we can hang at the Watchtower together again!" I beam, my eyes watering.

*****

Sunlight blazes on my left arm as I lay on the carpeted floor of our sunken living room, my nose an inch from the sliding glass door. Yellow, orange, and red leaves scuttle around our concrete patio, scattered by sporadic gales of wind, and I watch their dance, yearning for excitement or purpose. Exhaling morosely and dramatically, I draw a frowny face in the fog from my breath.

"I'm so bored," I pout and grimace moodily.

Rolling onto my side, an idea springs to mind: I should get drunk. My family has left for the weekend to visit my step-relatives, and I have the entire house to myself. Why didn't I think of this sooner?

Leaping from the floor, I bound to our kitchen and fling open the pantry door. Hoisting myself on the bottom shelf and leaning against the door frame, I select a massive, gleaming bottle of Southern Comfort.

"Hello, old friend," I chortle, jumping to the hardwood kitchen floor. *"Hello, old friend!"*

Several hours later, in the early morning, I sit in my bathtub, fully clothed, bawling and screaming while clutching my mom's senior portrait. She smiles affectionately from the frame with her shiny auburn hair and big blue eyes.

"I don't understand death!" I cry. "I don't understand God! Why would

He make death? Why would He make it so that we can never see each other again? Where's the fucking point in *that*? Huh? Is there anyone out there to answer me?"

My throat is raw and I hiccup miserably. Resting my mom's senior portrait delicately on the edge of the tub, I pluck my glass of Southern Comfort and Coke from the floor and take a gulp.

"Damn it! Damn it all to Hell, I say! And I say it again, now! Again and again, damn it all to Hell! And I can't *ever* tell Dad that I'm gay," I slur mournfully. "I can't break his heart like that. He's barely healed since you died, Mom. None of us have really healed. And there's no one for me to talk to. There's no one for me to tell that I'm scared. Dad can't handle all this on his own, and it's so unfair that you died! I hate God for killing you, for killing our family! I hate Him! I hate Him for sending a stupid woman to marry Dad! She's not *you*, Mom, and it pisses me the fuck off! Why would God *do* all of this? Is he really the Devil in disguise, and we're just all fooled?

"And—but—you know what? I've never really believed in Him. There, how about that? I mean, maybe I have. A little. But not the God of the churches. Not that evil, hating, vengeful and elitist God. But I do believe in some sort of 'God,' or 'Gods' or I don't know! And *that's* why I'm so mad. I'm so mad at Him or Her or Them or whatever They want to be called because They made me gay, They took my mom away from me, and They gave me the desire to do something great with my life, to be someone, but no clue how to do it. And it burns within me brighter than the sun! But I don't know how to handle all of this, I don't know how to handle all this desire and anger and sadness and obsession and pain."

I grab a bottle of shampoo and hold it to my chest.

"Sometimes I feel like my dreams fuel me, and sometimes I feel like my dreams weigh me down. Sometimes I just want to be a normal teenage boy who likes girls, gets annoyed by *both* of his parents, and only cares about football and video games. God, sometimes that sounds like a fucking *dream*, you know? To just be normal like that. Whatever normal is, I guess. To fit in? I don't even know."

Swirling the tiny bit of remaining amber liquid in my glass, I begin to chuckle and smack my lips loudly, blowing raspberries and singing nonsense in my falsetto.

"Oh, holy hell! I'm drunk. I'm drunk as a skunkity skunky skunk! Oh yes, Fiona dear," I prattle with a terrible imitation of a British accent. "I do quite thoroughly enjoy this boozy-booze feeling! But I've been rambling to my mom and the *toilet*. Although, I must say, you're a very good listener, Mr. Toilet. A *very* good listener. However, you do eat poop. You're like, 'nom, nom, nom—I *love* to eat *poop*! Farty poop, yes!' But listen, it's okay, I'm not judging you, I promise! Someone has to, Mr. Toilet. Someone has to. And even though we have never spoken before, I felt very comfortable talking with you, and I do feel better now, after saying all that. So, thank you, I guess, for letting me come out to you, Mr. Toilet. I am forever in your debt."

Shaking my head with a grin, I finish the last of my Southern Comfort and Coke, toss the shampoo bottle near the drain, wobbly rise from the bathtub, and plod to my bed. Within minutes, I am passed out, the oscillating fan on my nightstand ruffling my bangs.

I awake to a dreary, stormy morning, the rain pattering against my windows, and a sore throat, as if I swallowed an entire package of razor blades. Licking my lips, I rub my temples and reflect on last night's emotional meltdown.

"Did I come out to my *toilet*?" I croak groggily, glancing at my alarm clock.

It is nearly eleven in the morning, and if memory serves me correctly, I destroyed our kitchen preparing and devouring a drunken feast before stumbling to the bathroom for a much-needed therapy session with my toilet.

Crawling from underneath my tangled sheets, I gently wander from room to room, silent and contemplative. Rounding the corner of the kitchen, I am met with a sink full of pots and pans, a stove covered in marinara sauce and burnt garlic, and a spilled two liter of Coke. There is a lingering odor of stale food, liquor, and cigarette smoke.

"What a disaster," I observe stoically, with absolutely no intention of immediately cleaning up my mess.

Meandering onto our back patio, I walk from the cool concrete to the vibrantly green grass of our backyard. Barefoot, I pinch several blades between my toes, gazing over the pasture. The sky is a dull, cloudless gray, a silken breeze scattering fall's first fallen leaves. I wrap my arms around my shoulders tightly and tilt my head.

"I was kind of a maniac last night, Charlie. You should be more careful when you're drinking. Maybe I shouldn't drink so much at one time. What would Mom say? And wasn't Grandpa Joe an alcoholic?"

A spasm of anxiety ricochets through my stomach as I recall horrific tales told to me over the years about my Grandpa Joe's last days, spent in a hospital bed, yellowing with cirrhosis and writhing in misery.

"Oh, my God, that would be awful. Nope, I definitely don't need to drink that much in one sitting anymore. It makes me too emotional and I'll probably end up like Grandpa Joe," I rationalize to myself. "No, that's not the way to fix anything, Charlie."

Nodding my head in agreement, I turn on my heel, relishing the wet texture of the grass, and enter my ransacked kitchen.

"Okay. Alright. Okay," I mutter, assessing the damage and opting to open the windows and let in the fresh autumn air. "Okay."

Chewing my bottom lip, I drum on the countertop of the island and flip on Natalie Merchant before beginning to clear away the clutter. Her soothing voice soars on the opening high notes of "Kind & Generous" and I bop around, singing with her while loading the dishwasher.

An unrelenting, foreboding thought clings to me as I clean: what if I *am* like Grandpa Joe? Could I be more careful than he was? What if, knowing the history of my family, and our propensity for addiction, I vow to stay one step ahead of booze? I love its power, and I love that it can banish my stress and pain, but I refuse to become reliant on that power or its calming effects. I refuse to let it run my life. Although, I wouldn't mind allowing it to settle my nerves when necessary. I wouldn't mind becoming good friends with booze. I wouldn't mind being a heavy drinker, just not an alcoholic.

"That should be simple enough," I decide, closing the dishwasher and humming along with Natalie. "Yeah. That should be simple. And I'll ask Colin what he thinks about all this drinking and debauchery. Maybe he will have some insight."

THE FROG NO MORE

*****

A drowsy sunset of amber, violet, and coral hangs in the sky, the haze of dusk sweeping over the pastures before our house. I stand at my window with my arms folded neatly behind my back, watching the horses and mules graze, and waiting for Colin to log on for our evening chat. I am eager to talk with him, to admit my drinking to him, and gather his opinions on a few matters.

My ears prick at the noise of Colin logging in to chat. Spinning on the ball of my foot, I take a seat at my computer desk and pull out the keyboard.

> *Charlie*: Hi, babe! How are you?
> *Colin*: Oh, not too shabby. How are you, handsome?
> *Charlie*: Well, TBH, I'm not doing great. And I'm very nervous to talk to you about this, but I've got to tell someone, and you're the only one I trust. I haven't even said anything to Jana.

I send the message, my hands shaking slightly, nervous about his response.

> *Colin*: Awe, babe, that makes me feel so honored and happy, but also worried—what's going on?
> *Charlie*: Okay, I'm just going to type it all out and get it off my chest. I've been drinking lately. Not all the time, but more than usual, and I'm starting to wonder about myself. Anyways, I wanted to know if you ever struggle with drinking or anything like that? And what do you think I should do?

After hitting the enter key, a sense of relief spreads over me. I have told another person my dirty secret. I have freed myself of the burden of hiding my frightening behavior.

And I would love to know Colin's thoughts, but he's taking longer than usual to respond. My heartbeat quickens and I fret he has developed an aversion to my moment of truthful release. Anxiously tapping the bottom of my keyboard, I agonize over whether or not to send another message when his reply pops up.

> **Colin**: Wow, Charlie, I'm not really sure what to say right now, other than I'm really disappointed in you. Don't get me wrong, I am sorry to know you're experiencing a rough time right now, but I *definitely* don't think drinking is a smart idea. At all. And when you say "more than usual" I have to be honest and tell you that I think that's a terrible sign. Why are you even drinking in the first place? You shouldn't be drinking! How long have you been drinking? How are you even able to get alcohol consistently enough to say something like "more than usual?" This makes me feel like there's a whole other part of you that I don't know about. It's like you've been keeping things from me, or lying to me. And I'm not sure what to think or feel right now, Charlie. I'm honestly not sure.

It is as though I have been sucker punched in the stomach, the wind knocked from my chest as if I've fallen from a roof. I swallow dryly, my hands frozen and hovering over the keyboard before rage begins to boil within me.

> **Charlie**: Well, good fucking luck figuring out your thoughts and feelings. Bye, Colin.

I fire off the message and immediately disconnect from the internet, shoving my keyboard away with a grunt.
  "What the fuck?" I huff, standing from my chair and furiously pacing my bedroom. "What in the actual fuck? Welp, never doing that again! Don't trust people with your heart and secrets! And damn it!" My chin quivers and tears sting my eyes. "Damn it! I *really* liked him."
  Falling onto my bed, I am racked with sobs and clutch my pillow, silently wailing, swearing off booze and boys for the foreseeable future.

Moonlight ripples on the water of our pond, my feet dangling from the dock as I take a sip of cheap red wine and hum a mix of "Nothing Compares 2 U" by Sinéad O'Connor and "Foolish Games" by Jewel.

"Guardians of the East, I broke up with my boyfriend, Colin. He hates me because I'm a drunk. He said he didn't know what to think or feel about me. And I guess I can't blame him because—oh, hell—*I don't even know what to think or feel about me*. I don't know, maybe I overreacted? It felt horrible to be disapproved of like that. It caught me off guard.

"But it's okay, it's fine. We just weren't meant to be, huh? And who needs him? Who needs any of it, when you've got loverly, loverly wine?" I chuckle, plastered.

After crying my eyes out over Colin and listening to Sinéad and Jewel's epic ballads of heartache, I crawled from my bed and snuck to the basement, breaking into a box of wine untouched since Christmas of last year. Zig-zagging down our drive in the chilly night air while nursing a bottle of sweet red wine, I gave myself a pep talk, deciding if a boy can't handle me the way I that am, then they don't deserve me at all. And people drink all the time; as usual, I'm worrying needlessly and acting overly dramatic. I'm not an alcoholic, I'm only fifteen years old, for fuck's sake!

"You need to calm down and enjoy the ride, drama. Calm down and enjoy the ride," I say soporifically with a swig of wine. "'Cause I'm sure it's gonna be one helluva ride."

5

A Colosseum Shit Demon

June 2004
Florence/Rome, Italy
New York City, New York
18 Years Old

The cobblestones shine brightly under the lamplight, our voices echoing vivaciously off the buildings lining the narrow lane. Antony, our tour guide, wraps his arm around my shoulder as we stumble through the sultry Florentine night, throwing his head back in laughter. I admire his square jaw and curly black hair.

"Happy eighteenth birthday, Charlie!" he smiles.

"Thank you, Antony," I say, wishing to kiss him on his stubbly cheek.

Chrissy, Sadie, and Devin flounder a few yards ahead of us, giggling and supporting one another across the uneven lane. I swing my arm around Antony's waist, shaking my head in wonder.

"This is amazing. And soon, we're headed to Rome! I feel like I'm living in a dream right now," I hiccup.

"How much have you had to drink tonight, you saucy boy?" Antony asks.

I grin at his British accent—"Scouse," as he calls it—and hope my cheeks don't betray the heat of a blush creeping up my neck.

"I'm not sure, maybe ten or eleven? Not *too* many, I don't think. I made some friends at the bar and told them it was my birthday, and they just kept handing me shots and drinks!"

"Maybe we'll leave that part out when we see Mr. Heath?" Antony winks.

"Oh yes, it can be our little secret," I reply suggestively, with a simper.

The dining area of our hotel glitters in the early morning light, sunshine beaming through a wall of sparkling windows. I take a sip of my mimosa and peruse the fruit and granola table, my head tingly. I don't feel hungry, although I am fairly certain I woke up drunk, and should probably eat something. But do I actually want anything other than this crisp, refreshing mimosa?

"Maybe a succulent cigarette," I decide, stepping through an arched doorway into a charming courtyard boasting a tiny fountain with an angel in the center, its head tipped virtuously toward Heaven.

"Ah, Italy," I coo in awe.

Fumbling for the lighter, my complete and utter state of inebriation surfaces. I am totally and unabashedly shitfaced! An eruption of giggles overcomes me as I carefully place my shooter of mimosa on the stone floor and light a cigarette. Craning my neck at the clear blue Tuscan sky, I exhale a cloud of smoke. This is *the life*! This is how life is supposed to be! Fuzzy, tingly, saturated, effervescent. My soul longs to stay in Italy forever, forsaking the United States and my dreams of acting, to instead wander lazily from one gorgeous city to the next, drinking fine wine, smoking smooth ciggies, and bedding gorgeous Italian men.

"What a life," I sigh lustily.

But wait. I've been drunk *a lot* on this trip. Is that bad? Is it bad a life spent traveling while pleasantly buzzed appeals to me more than anything else in this world? Think of the art, the culture—the parties, the experiences, the glamour!

"Have you eaten yet?" Devin asks from the doorway, rousing me from my fantasy life. Morning sunlight shines brightly on her shoulder-length auburn hair.

"Nope, not yet. I was too thirsty," I counter cheekily.

"Oh? You've been very thirsty this whole trip," she quips, arching an eyebrow.

"You know, I was *just* thinking that! Do you think I've been drinking too much? I mean, I haven't blacked out. Well, maybe that one night in London, but I remember most of the musical we saw in the West End. It was called *Blood Brothers* and some lady kept singing about Marilyn Monroe. See! Ha, I remember!"

Devin leans against the door frame, crossing her arms over her chest with a smirk.

"Okay, but you *have* been drinking each night, you know? It's Europe, though, right? I mean, we've all been partying more than usual. It's just, you *are* drinking more than most of us, but you seem to be having a lot of fun," she shrugs.

"Hey, I haven't been drinking as much as Kevin from Phoenix. *And* I haven't thrown up anywhere!" I say proudly.

"Yet," she retorts with sass.

"Like you said, I'm just having fun! But, yeah, you do have a point, I should probably tone it down. Besides, I'd like to be sober for Rome and Vatican City. I mean, can you imagine going to the Vatican *drunk*? With my luck, I'd run into the Pope, hammered!" I cackle.

"That's highly unlikely, but it *would* be funny," Devin says. "Now come on, you should eat something, we're walking around Florence all day and visiting the Duomo, remember? You've been so excited to see the Duomo."

"You're right," I agree, snubbing my cigarette and shaking out my arms. "I feel so bubbly! Like a walking champagne bottle! And I'm seeing little black specks! That's new!"

"Yeah, you *definitely* need to eat," Devin chuckles, ushering me inside.

*****

I walk briskly ahead of our group, sweat dripping from my forehead and excitement fluttering in my belly. The Colosseum should be just around this corner, Piazza del Colosseo. Rounding it, my breath catches.

"*Wow*," I breathe in veneration.

THE FROG NO MORE

The myriad of its stacked arches catches the light gloriously, my eye following the many layers and curves of its architecture. I am consumed and awe-struck. A stillness settles over my body and I relax, my senses becoming hyper-aware, intent on firmly imprinting this moment in my memory. The heat of the sun blazes upon my head and back, bright and hot, and a faint breeze ruffles my shirt and hair. There is the usual smell of a crowded place, an aroma of cooked food, perfume, and the musk of mixing bodies. Noises of foreign tongues, shouts, and bursts of laughter fill the air. How many millions of human beings have scurried up and down this stone piazza before the Colosseum, bathed in shade from one of the oldest arenas in the world? How many have stood as I stand, enraptured at the moment and overcome with a deep love and appreciation for humanity's collective experience?

"Clinton students!" Mr. Heath's voice calls above the cacophony of Rome. "Over here, Clinton students!"

I pull myself from my trance and file behind Devin and Sadie, awaiting further instruction.

"And right over there, on that block, there used to be a statue, of some emperor, I think, and the gladiators would kiss it before they fought!" exclaims a boy from the Phoenix group, his curly red hair stuffed underneath a grungy baseball cap.

"Are you sure? I feel like you just saw that in the movie *Gladiator*," says Kevin from Phoenix.

"I think it's true!" the red-haired boy squawks. "I mean, I know there was a statue at least!"

"Clinton, follow me," Mr. Heath booms, turning to enter the Colosseum. "We'll go through here, then you all are free to roam for about forty-five minutes or so. Be respectful and polite!" he warns ardently.

Devin and I break away from the group and wander the circular walkway into the heart of the Colosseum. Leaning against a guard rail, I turn to look at her.

"I think this is the most meaningful thing I've seen so far," I say, glancing over the arena where gladiators once fought for their lives; where lions, bears, and giraffes were chained and used as a means of gory entertainment.

A COLOSSEUM SHIT DEMON

"How so?" she asks, gazing at the remnants of seats, carved and worn by time.

"It's hard to describe. It's almost like an eerie feeling, but in a good way, you know? I guess it blows my mind that this has been here for almost two thousand years. Like, two thousand years ago, someone stood right here, right where I'm standing, when it was brand new. There would have been a first event held here, *two thousand years ago!*" I utter fervently.

"Okay, I get it, it's old!" Devin laughs.

"It's *so* damn old! And it's mind-boggling that it's survived all that time!"

"I know what you mean. I've felt the same way all day today, while we've been exploring Ancient Rome. It's wild to think we've been around that long. And learned relatively nothing about living humanely," she says offhandedly.

"Very true," I nod.

Sunlight pierces through a high arch of the Colosseum and descends on the ruins of the arena floor, now jagged walls of stone and wood. Dozens of spectators are scattered across the tourist level, snapping photos or standing in mystified astonishment, myself included. I yearn to feel the texture of the stone seats when my stomach begins to flip, rumble, and gurgle.

"Uh-oh," I whisper nervously.

"What?" asks Devin, peering over the guard rail.

Pain strikes the center of my stomach, above my belly button, and spreads to my lower back.

"I think I'm about to shit my pants!" I groan.

"Seriously?" Devin whips her head toward me with a cackle.

"*Seriously!* It just hit me! Maybe I was feeling too many emotions? I don't know! But I *do* know I've got to find a shitter *right this minute*, or things will get ugly!"

"I think there's some near the entrance," she says, spinning on her heel. "Come on!"

I clench my butt cheeks and follow her, praying my ass doesn't explode on our way to the bathroom. Heat barrages my body, my shirt sticking to my chest and shoulders with sweat.

"Oh, no, Devin! *It hurts!*" I whimper.

"We're almost there, I think they're like little porta-potty things!" she says sympathetically, then gasps. "Damn it! Can you hold it just a little longer? It looks like there might be a line!"

I squint to where she points, agony spilling over me.

"There are *six people* in line! Devin, poop is about to fly out of my ass right here, right now! I can't projectile shit all over the Colosseum! What would they do to me if I did that?"

"Well, maybe," she says, stepping closer to the row of porta-potties. "Ope! There's a vacant one, but you'll have to pay!"

"Fuck it, I'll pay! That's fine by me! I don't have a choice right now!"

Jamming two Italian coins into the porta-potty receptor, I step inside and hold my breath. Water swirls endlessly in the filthy bowl beneath me, the toilet seat covered by human excrement and dried piss.

"Nastiness of the absolute nastiest! Oh, nasty as fuck!" I gag, unbuttoning my pants. "Okay, I'll hover my ass over the seat like this, and—and, *oh my Lord*!" I scream, my stomach cramping and then releasing the toxic poison within me.

A few moments later, I stumble from the row of Italian porta-potties and take deep gulps of fresh air. Devin guffaws from the stone wall opposite.

"Feel better?" she asks with concern.

"I think I gave birth to something dead in there," I say earnestly. "But yes, I do feel better now. I think it was all the booze and greasy cheap food I've eaten!"

"That makes sense. Welp, now that you're feeling better, wanna take some pictures? We've still got about twenty minutes left to explore."

"Yes! That's an excellent idea! Only, not of these porta-potties. Pretty sure I'll remember them for the rest of my life," I grin.

"You *were* in there for a while."

"Listen!" I snap playfully. "The water in the bowl never stops running, I had to hover, and I was birthing a shit demon!"

"A shit demon!" she cackles, doubling over with laughter.

"Yes! A Colosseum shit demon!" I chortle, rubbing my stomach. "I need to stick to fish and salad and water for a while, that's for damn sure!"

"No more wine?" Devin asks, wiping a tear from her eye.

"Maybe a glass or two of white wine at dinner, but no more. My stomach is an acidic cesspool. I guess I didn't realize that could happen!"

Devin snickers with a sideways glance, pulling her silver digital camera from her bag.

"Come on, you Colosseum demon shitter, let's get some pictures."

*****

The haze of twilight covers the sky, a blazing triumph of cobalt, lilac, peach, and amber. It is the perfect saturated lighting for illuminating the majesty of the Trevi Fountain. I stand dead-center of the carved masterpiece, thunderstruck. Having wandered here by my lonesome, I will most likely catch serious trouble when returning, but I simply couldn't stop myself. Italy is ancient, lively, and immensely soothing, evoking a sense of reverence within me that must be obeyed. I *must* walk the streets of Rome by myself, to see, taste, smell, hear, and touch the city on my own. Besides, I became a man in Florence upon turning eighteen and yearn for an epic moment reflecting on what that means, and what better place to do that than the Trevi Fountain in Rome?

The crowd has died down, with many people away at dinner or catching a quick nap. Scattered tourists snap photos and toss coins into the rippling water, fawning and giggling. Fishing a small Italian coin from my pocket, I press it between my fingers, contemplating.

"Whatever shall I wish for?" I say under my breath, rocking back and forth on my heels. "A life of choice," I whisper, flicking my fingers and sending the coin glinting into the air.

It crests before a statue of a man attempting to capture and tame a rearing winged horse, a pegasus, among a herd of winged horses. My eyes roam over the entirety of the fountain, suddenly aware of the scene depicted. Why are these vicious, muscular men capturing these innocent pegasi? Oh, why didn't I bother to brush up on my history before traveling to Europe? I had a whole year to learn!

I continue my study of the Trevi Fountain, and it seems as if these men are directed by a tall adonis with a bushy beard, wearing fabric wrapped around his midsection. Their faces appear young and cherubic, yet their actions are garish and domineering. I am swept away by the ornate detail in the wings of a charging pegasus, and the billowing cloth of the bearded adonis, all made of carved stone.

Two ladies, their hair crowning their angelic faces, stand behind the tragic scene, one clasping a thin spear while the other casually holds a cornucopia, water flowing from a vase tipped at her feet. While I have no idea what the hell any of these statues symbolize or represent, I am overcome with an epiphany of gratitude. At this moment, I understand life is bigger than the stage, acting, winning Oscars, and finding fame. I see underneath my ambition of becoming a lauded actor to its very root: I want the power to experience moments like this for the rest of my life. I do not want an average, encumbered life. I want a spectacular, remarkable life; a life overflowing with adventure and discovery.

I have the urge to bow, expressing my appreciation for the fountain and this moment, but decide to rest my right knee on the fountain's ledge instead. Crystal-clear water shimmers under the bright spotlights of the night, creating a misty rainbow.

"Please don't let me be a nobody, stuck in the middle of nowhere, poor and miserable. Please don't let me be a dud, or give up on myself. Please give me the courage to always take care of myself, to make something of myself. To be someone my mom can be proud of," I say desperately, barely audible above the roar of the fountain. "To be someone *I* can be proud of."

Fear holds significant sway over my life, and it's high time I acknowledged it. I am governed by fear, from my sexuality to the expectations of my future life. How did I become this afraid? Have I been pretending to be happy and "okay" ever since Mom died? *Am* I "okay?"

Surely I am, for I want for nothing, and if *anyone* should be emotionally damaged, it's Brod. *She's* the one who was practically a baby when Mom died, not me. I was lucky enough to spend thirteen years with Mom, while Brod barely got six. I'm healthy, young, relatively handsome, and intelligent—the world should be my oyster, although I can't help but feel something dire looms ahead, an unabating presence of gloom I haven't been able to shake for *years*.

Shivering slightly despite the balmy evening, I notice the crowd surrounding the fountain has grown completely sparse, and resolve to head back to our hotel. Stretching my arms above my head, I yelp in satisfaction and turn toward the pristine water for one last look.

"*Fly*, pegasi," I murmur devoutly, "and take me with you!"

I meander by the Palazzo Poli, an old aristocratic house, carefully brushing my fingertips against its exterior walls, gritty and textured. Night has fully descended, streetlamps and lighted shop windows glowing rosily. I catch snippets of Italian conversations as I traipse the streets, their language as beautiful and energetic as the city itself.

Pausing to lean against an arched doorway, I survey a balcony overlooking the street and vow to remember the magnificence of this moment for the rest of my life. I vow to myself, on all that is grand and wondrous, that I will take care of myself, no matter what. I will never let myself fall into the abyss of bitterness and despair. No matter how grievous my life may grow, I vow to always reach for the light and beauty of life. I vow that if and when times are tough, I will remember how full of life I felt while walking the streets of Rome, the Eternal City. I vow to live for myself, and to have a hell of a time doing it!

*****

"I'll have a vodka tonic, please," I say boldly to the flight attendant of our British Airways flight from Rome to London. He cocks his head slightly, wearing a cheeky grin, before handing me mini bottles of vodka and tonic water.

Catching Devin's wide eyes across the aisle, I shrug indifferently.

"Technically, I can drink until somewhere over the Atlantic since the legal drinking age is still eighteen and we're in international waters or airspace or some bullshit like that. Isn't that *great*?" I beam.

THE FROG NO MORE

She rolls her eyes and resumes reading *Harry Potter and the Order of the Phoenix*. Satisfied, I mix the vodka with the tonic water and take a sip. A bitter, acidic taste fills my mouth and I swallow hastily.

"Wha-cha-cha!" I breathe, undeterred, and take another sip, my stomach pleasantly seared. Smacking my lips, I decide to get obliterated before I'm cut off midway across the Atlantic.

Devin shakes me awake and prods my arm with her fingers.

"What?" I mumble groggily.

"Come on, we've landed in New York City! Hurry up, we've got to get to our connecting flight!" she whispers urgently.

"I feel like death," I moan.

"You shouldn't have drank so much," she replies reproachfully.

"Yeah, yeah," I say, rubbing my head and standing to grab my bag from the overhead bin.

"I've already got it, come on!" Devin hisses.

"Okay, I'm coming! And thanks!"

My ears ring unnervingly as we scamper through LaGuardia Airport, a spell of dizziness assaulting me. Devin strides ahead and I reach for her shoulder.

"Slow down," I gasp for air. "I think I'm going to pass out. I'm getting tunnel vision."

"Oh, good Lord, Charlie," she sighs, slowing her pace and handing me a bottle of water. "Here, sip this. And I guess we don't have to run like banshees, we've still got a bit of time."

"Thank you," I wheeze.

"Damn, you *are* very pale right now!"

"I'm telling you, I'm death warmed up."

Devin shakes her head and rummages in her purse for crackers.

"I shouldn't have drunk on the flight, okay?" I admit, shame and embarrassment pecking at me. "I drank so much on this trip, and I'm really starting to feel the aftermath. I feel puny. But I know *I'm* the one who did it, okay? So please go easy on me right now."

She relents, her face softening to become warm and understanding. "Alright.

Okay. Here, munch on these and maybe you'll be able to rest on the flight back to Kansas City."

"Thank you," I say genuinely. "And I promise I won't drink for a hot fucking *minute*."

6

Wine, Cigs, & Feathers

June 2005
Clinton, Missouri
19 Years Old

Pouncing into my sunken living room, I open the windows and spin in circles, pausing to peek through the glass storm door of the entryway. Our motorhome ambles down the drive, carrying Dad and Brod, my stepmom Letha, and my step-brother Ryker on a two-week adventure across Kansas, Colorado, New Mexico, Texas, and Oklahoma. The house is mine, and I intend on smoking a cigarette in the formal living room, thank you very much! Marvelous! But, I should probably make sure they actually hit the gravel road and top the hill before lighting up.

Teetering on the step of the living room, I watch as they crest the hill and disappear from sight, then bound to my room for my hidden pack of cigarettes. Giddy with excitement, I twirl around the pillars of our living room and light my smoke, a devious and rebellious spirit consuming me.

"Now for a spot of wine and some cheese! Oh, happy lovely!" I giggle and clap merrily, creaking open the wooden doors of our entertainment center and turning on the movie *The Four Feathers* to play in the background whilst I party.

Grabbing an elegant wine glass from our kitchen, I pour a stout cup of

Sauvignon Blanc. The biting, fruity scent fills my nostrils and goosebumps break out over my body. Sweet red wine is my usual choice of wine, but it seems white wine might be more refreshing. Nervously licking my lips, I bring the glass to them and let the wine flow over my tongue. It's tangy and crisp, with a twangy aftertaste.

"Hmm," I smack my lips, taking another nip. "Hmm. Mm. Mm. I don't like it. Nope, not even a little bit. Why do people make wine seem refreshing? But I guess one doesn't really drink for the taste, huh? One drinks for the effect."

Holding the glass of wine to the sun, I swirl it, bewitched by the ribbons of alcohol floating through the pale golden liquid. Maybe it needs to "air out?" Is that what it's called? Spinning a dashing circle, I wiggle my hips and swirl the wine, then take another sip.

"Nah, still nasty. It's like I'm drinking a liquid that manages to taste dry," I cluck my tongue and shrug, gulping half the glass.

Drumming boisterously on the countertop of the island, I decide to chug another glass of wine, then refill it to the brim, and head outside. Sunshine explodes magnificently and the weather is absolutely exquisite, the sheer perfection of a mid-June morning. Birds of all colors chatter splendidly from the trees of the meadow as if I'm in a Disney movie. I breathe deeply, relishing the scents of nature: honeysuckle from the fence line, our thorny rose bush, fresh earth and grass, vibrantly green and intoxicating, and the musky hay behind the barn. Stepping from our concrete patio to the grass, I expand and close my toes in the blades, cool and soft under my feet.

"'Tis a magical day, 'tis it not?" I coo, closing my eyes and facing the sun, spreading my arms wide to better absorb its nourishment. "Careful—don't spill your most precious potion, boy," I whisper.

Keeping my eyes closed, I bring my wine glass to my lips and drink deeply.

"You know, I do believe it gets better the more you drink it. Perhaps that's why it's called an acquired taste?" I observe, opening my eyes and peering around.

My stomach burbles pleasantly from the wine and I grin. Drinking never ceases to brighten the world, a trick that has delighted me since childhood.

The leaves of the trees and bushes are greener, the sky a more brilliant and striking shade of blue, the meadows and pond lush and luminous, all more vivid than ever before. It is as if the wine has heightened my perception of nature.

"As if I have vampire's eyes but can walk in the daylight!" I exclaim joyfully.

Dixie lopes across our backyard, her tongue flopping from side to side, then circles me, sniffing and sneezing.

"Hi, girl! Wanna go for an adventure?" I ask, draining my wine and petting her sleek summer coat, shiny and smooth.

Placing my wine glass on the brick steps of the patio, I clear my throat and begin walking down our long driveway. The asphalt is worn, cracked by decades of tires, faded, and crumbling, but I adore our driveway. It is flanked by two rolling pastures and winds down the hill our house sits upon. Dixie trots behind me, stopping now and then to smell the ground.

Strolling to the end of our drive, I stand in the middle of the gravel road. Stately oaks and walnuts tower over it, providing patches of delicious shade. Turning in a circle, I savor the sights and sounds of the country, a sense of tranquility washing over me.

"I am most certainly a country mouse," I mutter, stepping back onto our driveway near the edge of our chipped and rusted white front gate. Much like the driveway, it was once a glorious front gate in its heyday, made of stout iron poles standing twenty-eight feet high, yet now bares the marks of nearly thirty years of neglect. Although, I believe it adds a rustic, finishing touch to our charming ranch house on the hill.

Resting my arms on the beams of the gate, I stare vacantly at our horses and mules in the pasture. Tucker, my retired show horse, lifts his head in my direction and snorts. Chuckling, I crawl through the front gate into the pasture. Tucker lowers his head and begins walking toward me.

"Hey, buddy!" I call jovially to him. "Coming to see me?"

He offers me another snort, then throws his big head over my shoulder as I hug his neck. Petting from the tips of his ears down to his shoulder blades, I plant kisses on his nose and face. He sniffs at my pockets and hands.

"Sorry, buddy, I didn't bring any treats this time. I'll get you some in a bit when we walk back up to the house."

He kicks the ground with his rear left foot in aggravation.

"You're so sassy!" I chortle, walking deeper into the pasture. "Come on, let's have us a lie-down. I think the wine is making me kinda sleepy," I yawn.

Patting Tucker's rump, I melt to the grass and lay back, sighing peacefully. Tucker lowers his head, sniffs my chest, then wanders off to nibble.

The noise of insects lulls me and I let my mind drift to Drury University. In less than two months, I will begin my freshman year of college, and to say I'm excited would be a major understatement. Freedom is on my horizon. Absolute and complete freedom to be *me*.

"Wait, I *will* be able to be myself," I breathe, rising with an epiphany. Tucker pauses his grazing to look at me. "I can be gay in college, Tucker! I can *finally* come out! And I'll do it on the very first day, on move-in day so everyone knows I'm gay from the start. I'm *so fucking sick* of pretending I like girls. I do not like girls that way. *At fucking all*. I'm as gay as they come!"

Standing in jubilation, I pat Tucker's head one last time and begin my ascent of the hill. Will I come out to my family, too? *Will I come out to my dad*? A knot of fear immediately manifests in my stomach, weighing me down. At the thought of telling my dad I am gay, I instantly begin to tremble and my mouth turns as dry as a desert. Why am I reacting this way? Am I afraid of my dad?

"Or am I still afraid of disappointing him?" I mumble, hopping the gate of the pasture near our side yard.

Ambling through the front door, I stop in the kitchen to drink wine from the bottle, then dart to my room for cigarettes. Fumbling with my lighter, I realize my lips and fingers are slightly numb, a result of the wine no doubt, and a sensation I rather enjoy. Striking a flame after several attempts, I light my cigarette and sit on the ledge of our sunken formal living room. The end credits of *The Four Feathers* roll, and I swipe the remote from the coffee table, restarting the movie and puffing on my cig.

Popping the screen off the window, I dangle my arm out and flick ashes, then snuff my cigarette on the outside wall.

"Oh, but maybe just a baby nap?" I burp, settling on our massive couch, adorned with Tenango embroidery, a Mexican style of embroidery that has nothing to do with my family heritage but was chosen for this living room nonetheless. It's probably highly inappropriate to have this in our home, but I doubt my dad's first ex-wife, Suzie, thought of that.

Roused by droplets of water trickling on my face, I blink open my eyes, befuddled.

"Oh, shit the bed!" I yelp, jumping from the couch and slamming the window shut. A storm rages outside and I clasp my throbbing head.

"Whoa," I moan, woozy and nauseous. "Whoa! I shouldn't have moved that fast."

Slowly moving to close each window, I groan and waver on the edge of vomiting. Glancing at the clock as I shut and lock the last window in the dining room, I notice it's past six in the evening.

"Holy *shit*! I slept for almost seven hours!" I gape, noticing the nearly empty bottle of wine on the island. "*You! You* are the culprit! So *this* is a proper wine hangover, huh? Oh, you're the Devil!"

My stomach rumbles and I lean back on the counter. Food. I need food and a soda. Rummaging through our refrigerator, I heat up leftover lasagna and pour a can of Coke over ice. Shoveling the food into my mouth and washing it down with Coke, I notice my hangover symptoms begin to evaporate. My stomach no longer gurgles, my headache is gone, and my wooziness has dissipated.

"Huh," I cluck, tilting my head with a dastardly idea. "Don't people drink Jack and Coke? Isn't that a drink people order? I feel like it is and I feel like we have some Jack Daniels," I utter to myself, searching among the liquor bottles on the top cabinet of our pantry.

"A-ha!" I declare triumphantly, dusting it off, for it doesn't appear anyone has touched these bottles in months. "So no one will miss a tiny nip. But, shit! Now I've cleaned the dust off of it! Hmm, guess I'll have to roll it around in the dirt a bit. No matter," I chirp, tipping the liquor bottle to my glass of Coke and filling it to the top. The smell of Jack Daniels is stronger than wine or Southern Comfort, flammable almost. "Well, I suppose it *is* flammable," I muse.

Exhaling bravely, I pick up the glass of Coke and Jack Daniels and empty it in one gulp.

"Hootie hoo! *Wa-cha-cha-cha!*" I rasp, riddled with spasms. "*That* is an awfully strange taste!"

Heat scorches my body, originating in my tummy and spreading to my limbs, neck, and face. It's as though I've been set ablaze. I lick my lips, wanting more, and pour another glass.

"Good day, sir!" I banter, raising the glass in a toast before sucking it down. "And a jolly good night, too!" I belch, rubbing my sizzling tummy. "Welp."

Sauntering to our sliding glass door, I lean my forehead against it and stare at the moon, a small crescent hanging low in the sky. My breath fogs the glass and I draw a happy face, giggling. A magical liquid has arisen in my life, erasing all anxiety, pain, boredom, and doubt. With a bit of alcohol, life is sunshine, lollipops, and motherfucking rainbows! Who knew? My dreams suddenly seem easily achievable, my destiny sealed, my acceptance preordained. I am one with the universe.

"Ooommm," I snicker, striking a pose of serenity in the reflection of the door.

Fighting the urge to do cartwheels, I sprint down our hallway to my bedroom, grab my cigarettes, and dash outside to smoke. Bursting through our glass storm door with my arms wide open, I welcome the starlight glistening in the night sky.

"The stars are alive!" I bellow, cackling as I place a cigarette between my lips. "Oh, what a joyous evening!"

As I step down our brick stairs, I am inspired to play a game of my youth.

"Hear ye, hear ye! I call upon the Watchtower of the East, the Guardians of Air, Gemini, and Mercury! Listen to my plea! Hear my call! I need to lead an artistic and creative life! My soul *needs* this! I need a fucking purpose so I don't destroy myself!" I plead and cough, startled by the intensity of my last statement.

Stunned, I swallow dryly and inhale another drag. Will I destroy myself if I don't lead an artistic life? And *why* do I feel the tiniest bit of a thrill at the thought of destroying myself? Do I have another personality, a deviant Charlie hellbent on destruction? The darkness has always called to me, beckoning glamorously with the promise of an exquisitely drowsy and twisted existence. Is that more aligned with who I am, with what I *truly* want?

"Fuck," I sigh, stretching out on the grass of our front yard. "Fuck a duck. Guardians, I think there's more going on with me than I know about. It's dizzying, almost. I think you should probably keep a watchful eye on me from the Watchtower. I'm scared the madness may thrive in the coming years, and I'll need constant vigilance. I, um, apologize in advance."

*****

The sun boils my body, and the air is still and humid. I lay in our backyard upon a faded blue sheet, suntanning and listening to the *Practical Magic* soundtrack on my portable CD player. Dixie rests on her side near me, and I reach out to pet her as "Nowhere and Everywhere" by Michelle Lewis plays through my headphones.

"Oh, pretty baby girl, can I tell you a secret?" I murmur, scratching her ears. "Lately, I've been feeling an old feeling, one that's been around since my mom died, and I haven't wanted to acknowledge it, but that's foolish. So, I'll share it with you, 'cause I know you won't judge me. You see, in the past, I have wanted to run away. I haven't felt this way in a couple of years, but it's happening again. And don't get me wrong, going off to college is really exciting, and I'm sure it'll help me become an actor, but there's still a part of me that wants to run away. It's a small part of me, but it's there, and I don't know if I should ignore it or not," I sigh.

Clouds drift by overhead as I pet Dixie and chew my bottom lip, sorrow welling in my chest.

"I can't help shake this feeling of being fake. As if I'm living some pretend life where I go off to college and everything is perfect and I'm happy and things are great. But, I mean, I *am* living that life, it just doesn't feel real, and I'm so mixed up inside. I'm so confused. But I just keep doing what I think I'm supposed to do because I don't want to let anyone down or disrupt anything. I don't want to let Mom down. I want to go to college and become a successful actor. I mean, I say all that shit, but do I really mean it?

"Sometimes I think I do. And sometimes I think I don't. Sometimes I think it would be easier to run away and join a traveling circus. I could become a carnie. I could drink and do drugs and read Tarot cards for people. Is *that* who I'm meant to be? Am I really a gutter rat at heart, pretending to be some fancy city mouse?"

Dixie lifts her head with a yawn and I chuckle.

"I'm sorry, girl, am I boring you with my usual dramatics? But I'm afraid to say this to anyone else. I was honestly kind of afraid to say it to myself, but it felt good getting it out. I just don't know, Dixie. I just don't know. I *do* want to go to college, and I *do* want to have fun and try to become an actor. But I'm overwhelmed by the pressure of it all, and I'm scared if I say that, or even think about it too much, I will fail. I'm afraid I'll psych myself out, and I really will end up a carnie, strung-out on drugs and bald."

A wave of demented laughter crests over me and I run my fingers through my hair. Pushing my sunglasses off, I rise to a sitting position and rub my eyes.

"Oh, Dixie," I collapse onto her chest, nuzzling my face against her as I pet her stomach. "Enough of all that talk, huh? I'll never get a boyfriend that way, huh? Do you think I should come out as gay once I get to Drury? Do you think that's a good idea? I talked to Tucker about it, and he agrees that I should. And I feel like it's gonna happen. I feel like a cute boy is gonna look my way, and I won't be able to resist myself. And can you blame me? I've repressed myself for years—other than that one time in the airport. But I feel like that doesn't count. And I think it would be nice to have a boyfriend. It would be so nice to have a boy to cuddle with and wake up next to. I want a boy to text me cute things, and kiss me.

"I think when I get to Drury, I should go for it, you know? I shouldn't hold myself back like I did in high school. I should be who I *truly* am, I should be *myself*. I should be brave and join a fraternity. I should embrace the funny, silly gay boy that I am. I know that college is a chance for me to be free, and I *have* to take this chance. This is my chance to show everyone who I really am, and I can't let it pass me by! I won't!" I holler defiantly. "I will be more adventurous, too!

"It'll start with joining a fraternity—that's extremely adventurous for me since I get so nervous around straight guys. And I want straight guy friends, too, you know? I want straight guy friends that know I'm gay and accept me for who I am and don't care. They'll know that we're just friends, and I don't look at them that way, or think about them in that way. They'll be my friends, my brothers. I've always wanted a brother.

"And, you know what, Dixie? I think I'm going to do drugs at Drury, too. Nothing too wild like meth or heroin—can you imagine? People say you can get addicted the first time you do those kinds of drugs, but I honestly don't think that makes any sense. One time? *One*? No, that doesn't make sense. But, that would be *horrid*—life as a drug addict," I pause, accosted by a flutter of sinister visions depicting my life in addiction. "Anyways, I would like to try the mild drugs, like acid and mushrooms and fun stuff like that. And what's that other one people always talk about? Peyote, or something like that? Who knows? Maybe I won't even drink anymore, maybe I'll just smoke weed and do acid and mushrooms and peyote. I dunno, girl. But I *do* know this is my chance. This is my chance to begin my journey to power. My chance to build a solid foundation for an epic life, and I've got to take it, or I'll regret it for the rest of my life!"

She sneezes in my ear and covers my face with kisses.

"Thank you, girl, I couldn't agree more! And I'll miss you so very much and visit you as often as I can. Promise!"

7

Adrift & Running Amok

Summer 2008
Clinton/Tightwad, Missouri
22 Years Old

My phone vibrates on the rug of the living room floor, undoubtedly another fraternity brother calling to ensure I'm ready to co-chair recruitment, or "rush," this August. I have avoided their calls for over a month, and have no intention of answering now. I'm far too busy drinking boxed wine, smoking weed, and enjoying my summer break to care a fig about the fall rush for my fraternity, Sigma Pi. While I do love my brothers and our chapter, I need a break from collegiate life. I need a break from life in general. I need, well, I'm not sure *what* I need, honestly. Other than more booze and a juicy fat blunt.

Draining my mug of Sauvignon Blanc, I spring from the couch and stand on pointe.

"Fa la la la la, *la la la la!*" I chortle, stooping to check my phone. "Ugh," I sigh. A missed call *and* a text message, but not from a fraternity brother. From *him*. No, I don't wish to think of *him* right now.

Shivering slightly, I fling my phone to the ground and putter to my garage for more wine and cheese, leftovers from a function my dad held this last weekend for clients of his. Something like that, I think, although it doesn't really matter. The only thing that matters is I was left with four and a half

THE FROG NO MORE

boxes of Franzia white wine and a platter of cheese and meats. Perfect and delicious for my summer of drunken laziness!

Or is it my summer of broody self-reflection? There is a nagging sense of gloom and dread within me, ever hovering in my peripheral. It stirs memories of days long ago, after my mom died. A mysterious, all-consuming presence that is both invisible and powerful. Whatever it is, I am caught in its clutches, dragged down to a blithering state of fear and pressure, wanting only to escape.

"Blithering," I say aloud. "Blithering idiot, more like."

Opening the door to our garage, I squint my eyes in the bright mid-afternoon sunshine. A warm breeze ruffles my hair as I twist the knob of the boxed wine, filling my mug to the brim. Shuffling out to the carport, I stand in the shade of an ancient maple tree and gulp half the wine, smacking my lips. The grass and leaves are lush and overgrown, swaying gently in the wind. Ripe apples and peaches litter the ground of our peninsula, St. Francis of Assisi standing watch amid the suffocating weeds at its tip. I carefully stroll the stone path that traces the peninsula's perimeter and stand beside St. Francis.

"Afternoon, chap," I say, resting my hand atop his smooth stone head, worn by years of rain and ice. "Busy day?"

A gale of wind rushes over the hill my house is built upon and down into the valley below, rippling the water of our small pond. I take another greedy sip of wine, my fingers roaming the texture of St. Francis' head.

"Well, *I've* been busy today. Busy avoiding a phantom feeling of some sort. It's annoying! It's like I almost know what's wrong, I almost know why I feel like the floor is falling out from beneath me, but I can never quite grasp it. It's always just beyond my reach. I used to think it was me wanting to escape, to run away, but now I'm not so sure. Maybe I'm not meant to know? Maybe I'm just being dramatic, and I'm actually delighted and at peace. I mean, honestly, what do I have to complain about?"

I tap his head, frown, then burst into a fit of giggles, gasping for air and crumpling to the soft grass. Am I drunk? Am I sane? I'm talking to a stone statue about my emotional distress. I suppose it is better than a *toilet*, though.

Should I call someone, a doctor maybe? Or a therapist? How does one even call those people?

A hawk roams the sky, high above where I lay, its massive brown wings gliding effortlessly on the wind as it weaves among wispy white clouds in the sultry blue sky.

"I wish to soar one day," I say quietly.

Dixie, my hound, steps onto the peninsula wagging her tail ferociously. Near-blind, she smells her way toward me, sniffing my ear and licking my face before plopping down beside me.

"Hey, girl," I say, reaching to pet her satiny brown, black, and white fur. "I've just been chatting with St. Francis, yet he remains stoic as ever. I think I'm very sad, Dixie. Or maybe there are issues I haven't dealt with or something? I feel like I'm supposed to be happy and content, that I *should* be happy and content, but I'm not. It's vexing, to say the least. Vexing. Hmm, makes me want to watch *Gladiator* and get drunk."

I rub a circular pattern over Dixie's chest as she nods off to sleep. Oh, what it must be like to be her, living in sheer bliss, without the need for chemical stimulants. Why do I want to get drunk and high all the time? Why am I *afraid* of being sober? This is not good.

But, like, seriously.

Stumbling from the couch, I crawl to my phone, ringing shrilly on the wall charger. Blinking my bleary, drunken eyes, I see it is *him* calling.

"Ugh," I groan, then answer flatly. "Hey."

"What're you doing?" he asks, slurring.

"I *was* sleeping. What are you doing?" I say blandly, swallowing my irritation.

"Wanting your cock," he moans.

I bang the back of my head against the wall in frustration.

"Not right now, I'm too drunk to drive. And you sound super drunk, too. Are you driving?"

"Nah, I'm at my barn. Come over."

"Are you listening to me? I said I'm too drunk to drive." I repeat, fully aware

THE FROG NO MORE

I've driven in worse conditions, but hesitant to degrade myself in these early morning hours.

"But I want your cock now!" he whines.

"Well, I'm sorry. My cock is indisposed right now," I chuckle darkly.

"What does that mean?"

"It means I'm drunk like I've been saying! Listen, call me tomorrow afternoon and we'll see if we can work something out."

"No good," he exhales dejectedly. "I head out to Nevada for a few days tomorrow, that's why I was wanting to see you tonight."

I sink to the floor, a devious and domineering spirit surfacing within me.

"If you'll give me five hundred dollars, I'll head over."

"What?" he laughs. "I don't have five hundred bucks on me right now, but I can get it to you when I get back from Nevada."

"Nope. Five hundred now, or nothing at all." I declare.

"You really only want my money, huh? Do you even enjoy the sex?" he asks, his tone wounded.

"Sure I do, the sex is great. I just don't want to work, and you happen to have a lot of money. I mean, I guess this technically makes me a prostitute, but I'm okay with it."

"Don't say that. Come over," he pleads.

"I can't. And I've got to go back to sleep now. I'm turning off my phone, okay? Call me when you're back from Nevada. Bye," I say, ending the phone call before he has a chance to speak and powering off my phone.

"Gah!" I shiver, tossing it onto the carpet. "I'm not right! This is gross and weird, but I keep doing it!"

Well, I'm awake and thirsty, why not sip some wine? Sluggishly rising from the living room floor, I shuffle through the kitchen, its lights still blazing, and hook my finger around the mug I left on the island. Carefully stepping down the steps of the garage, I fill my mug full of wine and walk to the edge of the driveway. The night is bright and glorious, a half-moon glowing in the center of the sky. A symphony of chirping crickets and croaking frogs serenades me, joined by the mewling of a baby calf from the pond, no doubt annoying its mother as she slumbers.

Treading lightly through the damp grass, I step onto our concrete walkway and amble to the gazebo. A faint summer breeze carries the scent of our rose bush. Hiccuping, I plop on the swing, setting it in motion with a thrust of my foot. Taking a deep pull of wine, I realize my cigarettes are in my bedroom.

"Damn it, they're miles away," I mutter, then scream in pain as my big toe is jammed in a rut of the wood and I crash to the floor, banging my face and chest. "Shit, my ass!" I yelp from the ground, wincing.

Dixie stirs from her bed on the side patio.

"I'm okay, girl. But the gazebo just fucked me up real good!" I chuckle, clutching my throbbing foot in my hand. Once the shooting pain in my toe subsides, I'll hobble to my room and smoke a cigarette on the front porch. I should make myself chug a glass of water in order to avoid a wine headache in the morning, as well.

"Little practicalities," I mumble, imitating Lestat in *Interview with the Vampire*.

*****

"You wanna get spun the fuck out?" Avery asks with a devious smirk.

"You mean meth?" I blurt.

"Yes, dinglefuck! Meth! You ever done meth before?"

"Once, a year or so ago. But it was with coffee filters, you know? The ones they use to strain the meth, or something like that, I'm not really sure. Anyways, we put them in water and drank it. They were *disgusting* but I for sure got spun!"

Avery throws his head back in laughter, stringy black hair falling to his shoulders. His beady black eyes twinkle as he pulls a long glass pipe from the console of his truck. I have known Avery my entire life and we recently reconnected as friends over booze and drugs. We sit in his beat-up truck with the windows down, sweltering in the heat of a July night.

"So, just hit it like a weed pipe," he explains, holding the flame to the bowl's long stem and sucking air. Cloudy white smoke swirls thickly in the bowl and he pulls it from his mouth, careful to keep his thumb pressed against the mouthpiece. "Here, hold the stem and hit it."

I take the meth pipe from Avery and put it to my lips. Inhaling deeply, I hold the smoke in my lungs for several seconds, then allow it to billow from my mouth.

"Did I just make a meth cloud?" I gape. "Holy shit! I just made a meth cloud!"

"You made a helluva meth cloud, boy! I'm proud of you!" he smiles, showing a couple of slightly rotted teeth.

I nod, running my tongue over my teeth. Is that going to happen to me now? What have I heard it called, "meth mouth?" My heart rate quickens and a wave of prickly heat spreads over my body. Swallowing, I light a cigarette and give Avery a sideways glance.

"Fire up another bowl for us, sir," I chortle.

"Happy to, sir!" he giggles. "Let me make my own meth cloud and then I'll reload the bowl for us."

"Happy lovely!" I cackle.

A sense of invincibility sideswipes me. A sense of pure, unfiltered, absolutely extraordinary invincibility spills from the top of my head to the tips of my toes. I am elated, electrified with insurmountable energy, and radiating perfect and unbridled joy.

"This shit's amazing," I marvel. "Absolutely fucking *amazing!*"

"Oh, yeah," Avery agrees. "I get so much shit done when I'm spun! 'Course, I never expected to be smoking a bowl with *you*."

"Oh? Why's that?"

"Goody-two-shoes Charlie Gray? Smoking meth with rich, goody-two-shoes Charlie Gray!" he banters with a guffaw.

"What?" I grin, rather perplexed. "Where in the hell did you get 'goody-two-shoes Charlie Gray?' I've *never* been a goody-two-shoes and *I'm* not rich."

"I dunno. When we were kids you never used to drink or smoke or anything, so I always kinda figured you were a goody-two-shoes," he shrugs.

"I never drank or smoked because I didn't want to. I hadn't learned how glorious those things were yet. But it was never me choosing *not* to do those things, I just didn't know about them yet. I mean, I knew you were all doing them, but I didn't know what they did. I was blissfully unaware. Trust me, had I known, I would have been right there beside y'all doing everything you were doing."

"That makes a lot of sense, now that you say that. 'Cause I remember you never seemed to care that we were doing it or tell on us. You just never did it yourself."

"Exactly. I wasn't curious until I was around ten or eleven years old. And I'm even more curious now!"

He turns his head toward me, furrows his eyebrows seductively, and looks me over while chewing on his bottom lip.

"You know, I've been kinda curious about *you* here lately. Let's smoke another bowl and see where things go," he smirks.

Thirty-three hours later, I sit cocooned in blankets upon the chaise lounge in my living room, my eyes dry and unblinking as I watch *Intervention* on A&E. Clasping my hands together tightly, I clench my jaw in trepidation and empathize with the woman on the television screen. Her gaze is vacant and glossy, many of her teeth are missing, and sores fester on her cheeks and forehead as she wraps her arm with a rubber tube and injects methamphetamine. A grin twitches on her lips as she pulls the needle from her arm, her head lolling around on her neck.

"Fuck!" I hiss. "That's going to be me shortly, I just know it. That is going to be my life! *Oh, what have I done?* I haven't slept in forever, I did all the meth in the world and my life is over!" I cry, pulling the covers over my head in anguish.

After torching several bowls with Avery, we moved to the back of his truck and fucked like rabbits for hours. As best as I can surmise, Avery is bisexual and enjoys having sex with anyone and everyone while on meth, even though he claims to be straight when not on it. Memories of our escapade flash in my mind and I cringe, crawling from underneath my mound of quilts and blankets.

Having sex with Avery makes me feel dirty and wrong, but not in a good way. It felt wrong at the time, yet I was so high and drunk, I didn't care. At the time, it was easy to push away my pesky thoughts of morality and friendship. Yet now, I feel gross, tainted, and cheap. I feel used. I feel used by myself. I used myself to escape from the loneliness and fear of my day-to-day life. I used myself to escape from myself.

"How cracked-up is that? Oh, how *wretched*," I lament quietly, standing from the chaise lounge. "Meth is wretched. Sure, the sex was great, but who the hell doesn't want to sleep? This is madness!"

Shuffling to the garage, I grab my fifth of vodka out of the freezer and chug from the bottle. Its icy sear coats my throat and stomach, and I drink until I am out of breath. Gasping, I pull the bottle from my lips and quiver. Surely that will put me down! I've already killed a pint of Jack Daniels and two bowls of weed, and hope this added liquor will lull me to sleep. I do not enjoy staying up for days on end. I do not enjoy meth. I enjoy booze and weed, and that's it. Case closed.

"Ugh!" I scream. "I wish I could fly away from all of this! I wish I could…I wish…I don't know what I wish! Maybe I should just have sex with Avery again and become a meth addict. Maybe I should give up on life, on my dreams, before they have a chance to disappoint me!"

Catching my fractured reflection in our garage window, I scoff and fold my arms across my chest.

"Calm down, for the love of God! Shape up. Sleep. And calm the fuck down! Life is fine, there's no need for all this nonsense and drama, dude! 'Maybe I'll become a meth addict'—good Lord, Charlie Gray! Get a grip, and quick! You're annoying the hell out of me."

Nodding curtly, I step up the stairs to the kitchen and walk briskly to my bed. Laying on my side, I close my eyes to the sunlight and force myself to focus on remaining still, quiet, and calm. I pretend I am a bird, gliding high in the sky. Eventually, all the booze will kick in and I'll pass out. And when I awake, I can move on from this monstrosity and use my time more wisely: I will concoct a spiderweb of lies for my upcoming semester at Drury. My disappearance has not gone unnoticed, although I am not comfortable telling my friends and fraternity brothers I've spent the entirety of our summer break drinking vodka, smoking meth, and getting arrested. I'm not comfortable with telling them the truth. I will come clean with Anne, but no one else.

A ball of shame bounces within me and I howl at the ceiling, fitfully throwing myself onto my back and pounding the mattress with my fists.

"Fuck!" I pout, whimpering. "Fuck it all!"

*****

Water laps gently against the rocky cliffs of Truman Lake, the tips of our toes grazing its cool surface. Lorna flicks her lighter, heating the shell of a blunt before setting it aflame

"So, when did you come out again? I know it was sometime after high school, but I can't remember," she asks, inhaling deeply as a lock of gorgeous, thick black hair falls across her face.

I pinch the beautifully-rolled blunt from her and inhale greedily.

"When I was eighteen, right when I got to Drury," I say, exhaling smoke. "But I didn't come out to my dad until I was twenty, although I know he suspected it for years."

"Oh, so not that long ago, then, huh?"

"Yup, not all that long ago," I agree.

"Were you scared?" she whispers, her hazel eyes clouded by anxiety, fear, and marijuana.

"Yes and no. I was afraid my dad would be sad or disappointed, but other than that, I didn't really give it much thought. I came out to my Aunt Trella and my sister—you know Brod—and my cousin, Tay, very early on, and they always supported me, so it was a non-issue between us, you know? And everyone in college was accepting. I had a very easy, very lucky experience.

"But I felt differently about my dad. I didn't think he would cast me out or anything like that, I was just *so scared* it would hurt him or disappoint him, and I didn't want to do that. Not after everything he'd already been through. I didn't want to be the cause of more pain. But I was worried for no reason, because my dad took it in stride, and nothing changed between us.

"But that concept—the idea of coming out—haunted me *for years* when I was a kid and teenager! It was awful, growing up gay and being so frightened all the time of someone finding out or saying something. I mean, you know exactly what I'm talking about. Always trying to hide it, but being really bad at hiding it because it's who you *are*, you know? Such a strange thing we had to do as kids—hide a part of ourselves. Society doesn't realize that it's harming *children* when it makes up these stupid notions of who we should love and who we shouldn't. No wonder we felt so conflicted all the time growing up. No wonder so many of us lose our minds. And they wonder why we're tormented. Idiots," I roll my eyes.

"Anyways, though," I take a long hit of the blunt and pass it to Lorna, "—yes, it's a *very* scary thing to do, coming out. But it will most likely be a very happy moment, too, once you actually do it. I'm not saying it will *definitely* be a happy moment, I'm just saying it most likely will be. I do have friends who had a terrible experience when they came out, and I believe there is a special place in Hell for parents like that. Is it your parents that you're worried about coming out to?"

Lorna takes another toke. "Yeah, my mom. I know she won't disown me, but I'm afraid she's going to be upset because she really wants grandkids. Like, really, really badly!"

"Well, just because you're gay doesn't mean that's no longer an option," I offer encouragingly.

"Oh, my God, you know what?" she giggles deviously. "We should have little gay babies together!"

"Oh! Wouldn't that be awesome?" I cackle. "The poor dears would be absolutely beautiful—your dark Filipino hair and my blue eyes, can you imagine? But, they would be utterly doomed!"

"Doomed as shit!" Lorna cries with peels of laughter.

"'And ne'er was there a tale of more woe than that of Juliet and her gay Romeo,'" I simper devilishly, breathing in a large drag from the blunt with a flourish.

Lorna lays back upon the rocks, plucking the blunt from my fingertips.

"Ah, Charlie, I'm so glad we're getting high and talking about this. It's been eating me up since before I can remember!" she exclaims.

"Dude, I fucking know what you mean," I say ardently.

"I just wish it didn't feel like such a big deal. I mean, you make it sound like it's not going to be, but that doesn't mean I don't *feel* that way," she bemoans.

"Well, sure you feel that way! We can't shut off our feelings just because they don't make sense!" I retort genially. "It's okay that you're scared. You're okay, friend, I promise."

"And like you said, I'm sure they already know. I'm sure they've known for a long time. I mean, I feel like it's pretty obvious I'm a lesbian, but who knows?"

"I wouldn't say it's obvious," I say simply. "I mean, you're just you. I don't feel like you present yourself one way or the other, but maybe that's because I'm gay, too."

"Maybe. I get that, 'cause you're just you, too. And it's not super obvious that you're gay, except sometimes," she says with a smirk.

"Shut up! What do you mean?" I pout, albeit wearing a cheeky grin.

"Sometimes you are sassy *as fuck*, and it's so gay!" she blurts.

My jaw falls open as I double over with laughter. "True! Fair!" I shriek. "But isn't it kinda sad that we're even having this conversation?" I say, my joy faltering. "What a world, you know? We've created a world where people sit around fearing that some part of them may be obvious—we're afraid to show even the smallest amount of vulnerability because someone may exploit it. Oh, wow, I'm high."

"You are high, but you're making sense," Lorna says. "Do you think that's why we've been so whacked out of our minds lately?"

"What do you mean?"

"When was the last time you were sober? *Truly* sober," she asks seriously.

"I mean, I woke up sober this morning," I evade, snickering.

"You know what I mean," she presses, turning onto her side.

"I do. Honestly, I don't think I've been sober all summer. So, probably finals week, in May, was the last time I was sober for more than a day. Two months ago, I guess? But this summer has been fucking *wild*, this summer hasn't been normal. I've done *so much* meth!" I state solemnly, frowning. "I hadn't really thought about it until now, but I've done a lot of meth and random pills this summer."

"Me, too," she groans. "And, Charlie, I fucking *like* meth. It's scary."

"Really? I don't care for it all that much, but it does help me drink more, so I guess that's a plus. I hate staying awake for days on end, all twitchy and jittery and shit."

"Hmm, it doesn't do that to me very often. How much are you doing?"

"I have no idea. I just smoke bowls with Avery," I admit.

"Avery is a dangerous person to be hanging around, Charlie. You know this. He's not like he was when we were kids," she warns, rising and stretching. "Be careful with him."

"I know, I know. But I don't think he'd ever do anything to *me*. We've known each other since we were toddlers!" I reply imploringly, wondering if I'm trying to convince Lorna or reassure myself that my risky behavior isn't as reckless as it feels.

"Well, I dunno if you can count on that or not, bud. Listen, I'm just saying that if I were you, I'd be *very careful* around Avery. Actually, if I were *you*, I'd stop hanging around Avery altogether. But it's your life, and I get that, too," she shrugs.

The air ruffles my hair and I gaze at the hypnotic, shimmering water of the lake. "I think I should take these last few weeks of summer break and chill out, calm the fuck down for a minute. I'll still drink wine and smoke weed, but I need to get ahold of myself before school starts again. I haven't talked to *anyone* from Drury since leaving in May, and it's almost the end of July. I'm sure Anne is wondering what the hell has happened to me," I muse, my mind adrift, the embarrassment of running amok these last couple of months overpowering my emotions. "Ugh, Lorna, life is so dramatic! All I wanna do is play and have fun and do drugs, but for some reason, that seems to make me feel worse."

"Hey, I don't want to hear it," she says pertly, nudging my leg with her foot. "I'm the one still stuck here working at Walmart, remember? I'm the one still losing my mind in this—what did you always call it? A village of shit?" she chortles.

"A *hamlet* of shit," I correct her. "Oh, Clintonia, the lamest hamlet of shit there ever was!"

"That's right—a hamlet of shit! Well, I'm still stuck in this hamlet of shit, so remember that when you get to feeling all sorry for yourself, pretty boy," she zings.

"Okay, okay, that's fair. But, no one is making you stay here, Lorna! You should move to Springfield! You wouldn't have to go to school, you could work down there, party down there!"

"I dunno. Isn't Springfield just a bigger hamlet of shit?" she shrugs.

"Springfield is glorious!" I say reverently. "Springfield is where I came alive, where I started being myself. Maybe it would be easier for you to come out if you moved there, too?"

"I dunno. Maybe. It's in The Bible Belt, though! It'd probably just be the same bullshit in a different town."

"Okay, Negative Nancy!" I chide, throwing her a goofy grin.

Lorna's eyes meet mine, dimmed with pain and regret, and I sigh, my grin vanishing. She pulls her shiny, thick black hair into a bun and stretches her arms above her head, her fingertips appearing to reach to the sky and graze a soaring buzzard.

"Don't let this town eat you alive, Lorna. You know it can do that if you let it. And you're such a force—you've got such a bright light in you, just remember that when you're feeling lost and hopeless."

"Yeah, well, thanks. And you remember it, too, 'cause that's true for you, too. It's even more true for you," she says, her eyes brightening.

"Oh, pish-posh! C'mon, bitch, let's get some snacky snacks, 'cause this bitch is friggin' *starving*!" I holler flamboyantly.

"*That*! That right there is when it's obvious you're gay!" she points at me and guffaws.

"Touché," I reply with a wink. "Touché."

8

Spun for Fun

Late October 2016
Springfield, Missouri
30 Years Old

My legs and arms twitch violently and I snap open my eyes, squinting in the bright daylight. A dull, throbbing pain pierces my temples and the front of my head, above my left eye. Swallowing, I struggle to lift the fog from my brain. Where am I? This isn't my bed, this isn't my room!

And it comes crashing back to me: I fell asleep at a random tweaker's house, and honestly can't remember exactly where I am. On the outskirts of Springfield, I believe, but in which direction? Oh hell, I've done it *again*!

Flinging the flannel sheets from my body, I discover I am naked, and glance blankly around the sparse room for my clothes. Brief images of showering in a tiny bathroom flash in my mind and I rub my face, standing. Head spinning, I walk toward a stained and chipped door, opening it cautiously to peer down a dim, wood-paneled and burgundy-carpeted hallway.

"Hello?" I call, my mouth dry from anxiety.

"Hey there, sleeping beauty," a man's head peeks from behind a doorway further down the hall. "I thought you'd never wake up!"

"Um, hi," I say, stepping out of the room and plodding down the hallway into a dingy kitchen, birthday suit and all. "I think we hooked up last night?"

"A few times, sexy boy," he chuckles, wearing green and yellow plaid boxers and nothing else.

"Where am I?" I ask, noticing empty liquor bottles, crackpipes, needles, overflowing ashtrays, and several bongs cluttering the countertops.

"Just outside of Springfield, close to Sparta," he answers, turning his back to me to scrape white power, which is surely meth, off the counter and into the bowl of a bong. "Wanna get spun out and fuck around again?" he jerks around, leering.

"I—uh, no thank you. But," I say, my mouth watering at the sight of a fifth of vodka, "I will take a few shots of *this*."

He giggles and lights the bong as I slam back four shots with a slight cringe.

"There, that should help," I whisper, leaning against the counter and closing my eyes.

"Oh! I was supposed to wake you up and tell you, but I got busy and forgot. Jeff borrowed your car real quick, to run your errand, but he should be back soon. He left over an hour ago."

"*What?*" I gasp. What the fuck have I gotten myself into? "Do you know where my clothes are?"

"Probably in the bathroom," he shrugs.

"Is this Jeff's house?"

"Yeah."

"I—he just *took my car?*" I gape, incredulous.

"You told him last night that he could use it today," he says evenly. "Remember?"

"No, not at all, but of course I did. Fucking *of course* I did! Why *wouldn't* my stupid fucking dumbass do that?" I shout, stomping down the hall and opening random doors in search of the bathroom.

"Dude, calm down, you're kinda freaking me out," he hollers from the hallway.

"I'm sorry," I groan, finding the bathroom and flipping on the light, where my jeans, t-shirt, boxers, and socks lay neatly folded on the sink. "I just don't remember much from last night, and *I'm* kinda freaking out!"

"You *were* pretty fucked up last night," he says, leaning against the door frame of the bathroom.

"I'm sure I was," I agree bitterly. "Listen, I'm also sorry to ask this, but what is your name?"

"Trenton," he smiles, the pupils of his green eyes pinpricks.

"Well, Trenton. I'm Charlie," I say, pulling on my boxers.

"I know that. And you should leave those off."

"Maybe later, Trenton. But right now, I want to drink some more vodka, smoke a cigarette, and calm myself the fuck down. Like, am I safe? Y'all aren't gonna do anything weird to me, are you? Is Jeff selling my car? You should know my family can see my location on my phone—they'll see that this was my last location and that I spent a long time here. And I have a *ruthless* backwoods family—they won't go to the police, so if you hurt me, they'll track you down and take you out. And trust me, it will *hurt* and they will make that pain *last and last!*" I snarl, my tone deep and vicious. I grab my socks from the sink and cast Trenton a defiant glare, sweat covering my body.

"Wow, dude! Whoa! Paranoid much? You *seriously* need to chill out, man! No one is gonna hurt you, but that *was* a scary speech you just gave. You turned scary quick, Charlie! I mean shit, dude—you fucked me three ways from Sunday last night, you don't have to be worried! And Jeff went to pick up some pills for you, but I guess you don't remember *any* of that, huh?" he says coldly.

"Hey! I'm *not trying* to be an asshole or threatening or weird, or anything like that on purpose. It's just that I really don't remember *anything*! He's getting me pills? What in the fuck?" I exclaim.

"You said you wanted some Xanax bars, and he knew where to get some, so he's off to get them," Trenton mutters simply. "We're actually very nice and helpful people."

"Shit, listen, I'm so sorry. I'm sure you are. It's just—damn it! It's like I need to be chained up somewhere," I muse, massaging my neck.

"Sounds hot," he grins and I chuckle dolefully.

"Well, Trenton. Looks like I'm here for a while longer. Let's get fucked up," I sigh, resolving myself to my fate.

"Will you do your scary man voice again? It was actually kind of hot," he giggles.

I roll my eyes and meander to the kitchen for another round of vodka shots.

Stumbling through the door of my apartment, I toss my keys and a pint of vodka on the coffee table and collapse onto my red couch. Sweat covers my entire body and my hair sticks to the back of my neck. Curling onto my side, I wrap my arms around my legs, absorbed by the heavy beat of my dehydrated heart as I gaze at the clear plastic vodka bottle, little bubbles frothing under its label.

"You're the Devil, you know that?" I say quietly and with malice. "You're the *fucking Devil*! But I love you."

By the time Jeff returned with my car, I had finished his fifth of vodka and smoked two bowls of his weed. Chemically ecstatic with myself, I suggested we snort lines of Xanax before parting ways. It is my last coherent memory until awaking in the back corner of my apartment complex parking lot, resting on Esteban's steering wheel with my driver door wide open, the sun scorching my left arm and leg. The chatter of squirrels roused me, and I noticed an unopened, shiny pint of vodka tucked safely in my door's pocket.

Where have I been? What have I done? No one knows.

Rising gently from the couch, I swipe the vodka from the table and shuffle to the kitchen, placing it upright on the countertop to settle. The clock on my stove reads five in the evening and I gather all of my mental focus, shivering. Have I been blackout for *two whole days*? And why is there a gash on my right elbow? Wincing, I tap the skin around the gash and sift through my memories.

Holding my wounded arm, I stare at the bottle of vodka as images begin to appear in my mind: there was an outdoor patio, and it was screened-in with fake grass on the concrete floor; there was an ancient brown folding card table and several metal chairs with grimy cushions. Where in the hell? And a hot tub! There was a large brown hot tub beside the screened-in porch, and it had a green cover that matched the fake grass. I opened the hot tub—*I got naked in the hot tub*! Dread and gloom break out over my body and I pound my fists on the counter.

"Damn it, Charlie!"

An image of a hazy, smokey den emerges, full of random people I can't remember, as we pass around a torch and meth bong. I required help in lighting the bong, and remember guffawing for hours with a girl on a saggy couch. April? Was that her name? How much meth did we smoke?

And the Xanax! A memory of snorting lines of Xanax and falling off a porch, but not at Jeff's house, or the house with the screened-in porch and hot tub, or the house with the den. Was it the same house? How many fucking trap houses did I visit in my bender? Do I even have any Xanax left?

"My shoulder is so sore, too," I mumble, twisting the vodka open and patting the pockets of my jeans.

Leaving the cap on the counter, and the vodka untouched, I rush to my keys on the table, out the front door, and down to Esteban, searching frantically for my baggie of Xanax. Locating it in a backseat cup holder, I count three and a half bars from my original seven. Popping the half into my mouth, I amble upstairs to my waiting vodka bottle. Its pungent scent sends quivers down my legs and I shudder, deciding to grab a jar of pickles as a chaser.

Closing the door of the fridge reminds me of running through a soggy embankment in the dead of night and jumping over an abandoned refrigerator, frightened yet exhilarated. Was I bounding like a *deer*? Did I *think* I was a deer? Shaking my head, I remember scurrying across the street to the parking lot of a Walmart, where Esteban was waiting for me. Why was Esteban waiting for me in a Walmart parking lot? Where are the rest of my memories? Lost in the void. Lost by lines of Xanax, blunts of weed, bowls of meth, gallons of vodka, and absolutely no food, water, or sleep. My poor body. My poor *soul*!

"Okay," I sigh dejectedly, rubbing my eyes. My chin quivers and I steel myself, breathing deeply through my nose and taking a sip of pickle juice before gulping four long swigs of vodka. "Holy bitches! Shit, that's *potent*!" I cough, placing it back on the counter. "Oh, I don't want it, but I do!"

My stomach gurgles and a shrill ring explodes in my ears. I clasp my hands before me, stand perfectly still, and chatter my teeth, fighting my body's urge to vomit. Several seconds tick by as I wrestle with myself, willing my body to keep down the vodka and Xanax.

"Keep down the vodka and Xanax, Charlie? Are you trying to kill yourself? That's *so* not a healthy trick," I observe after ensuring my body will not reject the poisonous duo. "Aren't you tired of this, Charlie? Aren't you tired?"

Days like this are what you live for! You love the darkness, the haziness! You love it and you know it, silly dumb boy! A sneering, snide voice answers from the back of my mind.

"I'm not a silly dumb boy! I didn't want to throw up and waste what little bit of Xanax I had left!" I retort. "But, maybe I *do* love it, a little bit. *Why*, though? What does that *say* about me? And why do I talk to myself as if there were three of me? Oh, this can't be a good sign. Good God, man! The drugs are eating you up!"

Stars twinkle through the sunroof of Esteban, the choir of singing crickets and frogs carried on the breeze. After nibbling on another half bar of Xanax and finishing my pint of vodka, I dragged my numb body to Esteban and slumped into his passenger seat. It's easier to smoke while sitting. Reclined, I exhale a cloud of cigarette smoke and yawn. Soon, I will need to go back upstairs to my apartment, to avoid suspicion, but for now, I am safe to finish my cigarette and stare at the night sky, contemplating my future. The lights of a plane flash among the stars as it flies over Springfield and I yearn to be one of its passengers.

"I think you should go to rehab," I remark, my eyelids drooping. "I think you have serious substance abuse problems, and you need to go to rehab. You should fly yourself away to another rehab, stupid boy.

"And I think you need to figure out something to do with your life, man!" I hiccup. "You need to be careful, or you're going to end up getting swallowed by the world of drugs. You're going to lose your teeth and your hair and probably die. But, like, *seriously*, Charlie! You're playing with the Devil, and as much as you like it, you've *got* to realize that it's super dangerous! You've got to get your head out of your ass before it's too late and you become a depressed, homeless, gutter rat basket case! You deserve so much better than this, you know that, right?"

I flick my cigarette out the sunroof and stretch, vowing to sober up and take a nap.

"Or I'm sending you off to rehab, you hear?" I slur, yawning again. "Shit, I ate way too much Xanax."

Rising unsteadily to my feet, I ricochet up the stairs, through my apartment door, and settle into my bed, careful to rest on my side.

"Sleep on your side, stupid boy, so you don't asphyxiate and die a tragic death! And to think, you were once the luckiest boy in the world. Santa, why hast thou forsaken me so?" I mumble, my eyes closing drowsily.

9

Affinity

October 2019
Yorba Linda, California
33 Years Old

I drunkenly untangle myself from the seat belt of Affinity Recovery's "druggie buggy," my jaw dropping to their pebble stone circle drive as I heave my bag over my shoulder. This is, *by far*, the swankiest, most luxurious rehab I have *ever* attended! Vibrant, leafy vines and immaculately groomed bushes adorn the grounds, blooming amid thick rosewoods and narrow cypress trees. A wall of lush, colorful flowers surrounds a regal, wrought-iron front gate, and a dome of windows with a partially patinaed copper roof looms in the distance. Shaking my head to steady myself, I push open the wrought-iron gate and gasp at a stone fountain, large enough to sit in and splash about, streaming in the center of a sunny, foliage-drenched courtyard.

"Wow," I breathe, gazing around the mansion and courtyard.

Floor-to-ceiling glass windows form a *U* around the courtyard, sheltering a lavish marble hallway with cathedral ceilings; a mural of gloriously detailed Tuscan pastoral settings spans the length of the various rooms, interrupted by four arched doorways. From where I stand, I see two spacious bedrooms, a side bathroom with an impressive stone-basin sink, and a library stocked with books, chaise lounges, and a stately pool table. My eyes wander the *U* to an outdoor patio, covered with a mossy roof and shielded from the elements by a heavy curtain draped elegantly beside a couch, two chairs, and a coffee table. The tasteful outdoor furniture is placed cozily around an enormous fireplace and mounted flat-screen TV.

"They have an outside living room!" I gape, awestruck.

"Charles?" a voice calls to my left, near the outdoor fireplace.

In the door frame stands a curvy woman with an oval face, lustrous crimson hair, and twinkling hazel eyes.

"Hi, that's me," I answer.

"Hello! I'm Tessa," she says, waving for me to follow her.

"This place is *beautiful*!" I gush, stepping from the patio to the hallway.

Tessa leads me through a foyer with a delightful two-story marble spiral staircase and broad windows overlooking the valley and houses below.

"Look at that view!" I exclaim, my eyes roaming across the backyard of the house, discovering another outdoor patio made of octagonal pale stones complete with a built-in grill, pristine and shiny, and an extravagant entertainment area. Paths of smaller octagonal stones wind throughout the impeccably manicured grass, while verdant bushes provide a buffer between the backyard and the edge of a steep hill.

"Oh yes, it is very serene here," Tess beams. "Would you like a tour real quick?"

"Yes, please!" I chirp, hiccuping.

"You're sweet, and still a bit drunk, huh?" she says simply, turning on her heel and walking into the *U*-shaped hallway. "No worries, remember what you can. We'll get you some meds and food soon. Now, down this side of the hall is the laundry room," she points to a slender room with four industrial washers and dryers and a countertop spanning the wall. "And here is the theatre room," she nods.

My eyes widen in excitement at the huge movie screen, framed by sleek red velvet curtains and an intricate sound system. Four rows of plush, blood-red movie theatre seats face the screen, five in each row.

"Holy shit! It's got real theatre seats and *everything*!" I marvel.

"Yup. And that door," she gestures to her left, "leads to the garage and out to the courtyard. And if we go back down the hall, we'll get to the kitchen. The primary bedroom and my office are up the staircase. You'll be downstairs, though, off the kitchen and library, on the other side of the hall. There are three bedrooms, each with two beds, so six patients total."

"Oh, wow, that's not many beds."

"Yes," she chortles, "this is our biggest house but sleeps the smallest number. You got very lucky getting placed here."

"Oh, yeah. I, um, told them I had to stay somewhere bougie or it was a no-go. It's just—I've been to *so many* damn treatment facilities, I really know what I'm looking for. I was drunk, but I think I literally told them if they couldn't put me somewhere fancy, I was hanging up. I can be a bit melodramatic sometimes, and an ass when I'm white boy wasted," I grin innocently.

"I'm sure you can," she retorts playfully.

Tessa brings me through a cupboard of sorts, full of tall cabinets containing cereal and snacks, into a state-of-the-art glimmering kitchen with more square footage than most homes. It is absolutely sumptuous: dark, rich wooden cabinets and polished granite countertops, expensive hardwood floors, and appliances fit for a palace chef. An inviting bay window sits snugly at the far end of the room, shaded by an ancient desert willow, offering a sweeping and spectacular view of the valley.

"Well, I'm certainly reading books right there on those cushions, yes I am," I say matter-of-factly.

"Quite the spot, huh? Come on, I'll show you to your room and then take you to the nurse. His office is at the end of the hall, where your bedroom is."

"Sounds good," I say.

Standing at the edge of the backyard, I lean over the long, narrow silver lupine bush and peer down the ledge. It reminds me of the cliffs of Truman Lake, and I can hear laughter and the voices of children playing in the streets of the valley below. Lights twinkle on the hillside across the valley, sublime and splendid mansions gazing at one another over suburbia.

"But no matter where you go, Charlie, there you are," I murmur.

Wobbling to the patio of the backyard, I delicately rest in a lounge chair, stunned by the outstanding view of the glittering valley below. The evening is growing late, and my meds are certainly kicking in, but I want one last smoke before passing out. Flicking my lighter, I see Vicente step out of the kitchen's side door. He is of average height, with light brown skin, short black hair, and impish brown eyes. He wears a neatly trimmed mustache and a perennially satisfied, smug smirk, and for some reason, I believe we will get along smashingly.

"Hey, Charles," he grins, sprawling across the stone steps and puffing his vape.

"What's up, Vicente?"

"'Bout to head to bed. Whoa—how *you* feeling? Your eyes look hella glassy, and your pupils are huge! You look like you're tripping, bro!" he chuckles.

"Oh yeah? People always say that to me when I'm taking detox meds, but it's probably all the Ativan. I'm not sure what I'm on right now, but it's a lot. Most of it was self-prescribed before I got here, and they're doing their best to wean me off," I shrug.

"Yeah, I was *so messed up* when I got here, man! So, you feeling alright? It's a tight group of us, bro. There's only six guys here at a time, and no one's been here that long. Bowen's been here the longest, a little over a week or something. And, obviously, there's lots of space."

"That's no joke. And I guess I'm doing pretty good right now. I think flying all the way to California helped. I feel like I left my old life behind, and I can start over out here, because I'm not going back to Missouri. I can't. I've *got* to stick with a program for once! I've got to do more than just finish rehab. I've got to move into sober living, do IOP—all the shit I've never done before, because I'm fucking *done* being a piece of shit alcoholic, dude! And like, sure, I got plastered on the flight out here, but I was having all these—these revelations—and connecting the dots, you know? Like, *actually* figuring it out, not spouting bullshit that sounds legit so I can impress people.

"I was *really thinking* during the flight. I was trying to trace this whole debacle—my alcoholism—back to its roots. And you know, I remember when I was younger, in my early teens, I would have these moments where I didn't know what I was feeling. And it wasn't an absence of feeling or feeling too much at once or anything like that. It was more like a set of feelings that I'd never felt before and I didn't know how to identify them. They would descend upon me, and it would make me want to run or be devious, or daring. It was like I wanted to escape, to be someone other than myself. Now, though, I realize it was just alcoholism, beckoning me from a very early and impressionable age.

"So, I guess if I'm honest with myself, my alcoholism really began when I was thirteen, shortly after my mom died. And here I've spent *all these years* convincing myself one thing had nothing to do with the other. But I see it clearly now. Those elusive feelings I couldn't identify were simply extreme grief, fear, and anger—to an extreme that I had never encountered before. Of course they seemed foreign to me! I had seen death in movies and on TV, and I had read about it, but I had never encountered it myself. I simply wasn't equipped. And, naturally, my brain was pre-disposed to escape using alcohol, and that explains why I was so drawn to it after Mom died. Mind you, I honestly didn't drink much, maybe seven or eight times over the course of a year, but I did use it as an alcoholic does. I used it to numb, to escape, to live in a world where Mom hadn't died, where I could pretend that life was just as beautiful as it had been when she was alive.

"And you know, I *liked* being courted by alcoholism. I *liked* having my emotions toyed with, I *liked* that it was vague and confusing. A part of me, that is. I just couldn't see it for what it was at the time. But then again, none of us can, huh? Otherwise, we wouldn't have addicts and alcoholics. And damn it," I sigh with a laugh. "Sorry, Vicente, I'm talking in circles. I'm talking your ear off."

"Shit, you're good, bud. You're on a lot of detox meds right now—I get it—but you were actually making a helluva lot of sense, dude. We don't know each other very good yet, but I think you might be on to something," he grins.

"We don't know one another at all, huh? But, I think you might be right," I nod, taking a drag of my cigarette. "I think you might be right."

*****

THE FROG NO MORE

"Hey, Charles," a handsome boy with curly auburn hair whispers from my door. A beam of sunlight strikes his face, highlighting his chiseled jaw, as I search for his name. Rowan, maybe?

"Yeah?" I answer groggily.

"You should wake up and eat some breakfast, it's almost nine. Groups start at ten. You feel alright?"

"Yeah, I'm alright. Thanks, man. I'll get up," I say, crawling from underneath the sheets.

"Right on," he smiles and closes the door.

Throwing on a fresh pair of shorts and a shirt, I quickly brush my teeth, pull up my hair into a bun, and head to the kitchen. Rowan, Vicente, and another guy with short brown hair and brown eyes, whose name escapes me, mill about the space.

"Morning, Charles," Vicente grins, tossing a cigarette to Guy Whose Name I Can't Remember as the two of them step out to the back patio.

"Morning," I yawn, grabbing a shiny Granny Smith apple and leaning against the kitchen island. "Rowan, right? I'm having trouble remembering names right now. And what's up with everyone calling me 'Charles?'" I ask.

"Yeah, I'm Rowan," he answers, his green eyes twinkling as he pushes a plate of eggs, bacon, hashbrowns, and toast toward me. "And that's what Tessa told us your name is. Is it not your name?"

"Oh, no, it's my name. I just usually go by Charlie. But, you know what? I kinda like it. New state, new me, I guess."

"Cool. And are you sure you don't want something more filling than an apple?" Rowan says, gesturing to the plate of breakfast.

"Oh, I probably should, and that does look delicious, but I'm still too early in detox to have much of an appetite."

"Feeling nauseous?"

"Nah, more like I'm not hungry, and eating would just make me feel sick. I'm pretty used to this whole detox thing. I've figured out the way my body works," I shrug.

"What are you detoxing from?"

"Vodka, mainly," I say.

"Another vodka man! Right on!" he yelps, clapping.

"Yeah?" I say with a timid smile.

"Yes, sir! Vodka and whiskey are my girls, but vodka will always be my first lady. I have fucked around with meth and heroin, but I'm mainly a good-for-nothing drunk," he chuckles. "Everyone else here is a drug addict, we're the only drunks! Nice to have some company."

"Ah, but we're *all* a mess," I sigh.

"This is very true," he agrees. "Where are you from, by the way? You have a bit of a Southern accent."

"I do? How fun! I don't feel like I do, but maybe to people from California I do? I'm from Missouri and grew up in the country. Maybe my twang is coming out? Probably 'cause I'm nervous."

"Missouri, huh? I've got a lot of family down in Arkansas!"

"Oh yeah? Where in Arkansas? I've got lots of family from there, too!"

"Fayetteville," he answers. "Is that where your family lives?"

"Nah, mine are all in Jonesboro. But I've been to Fayetteville, and it's beautiful!"

"It sure is. Why are you nervous, bud?"

"Shall I count the ways?" I laugh darkly, shaking my head. "I'm just on high alert, I guess. I flew halfway across the country yesterday, drunk as a fucking skunk, and I haven't told my family yet. They probably still think I'm at my apartment in Kansas City. And I'm gay, and usually a bit leery until I've had a chance to gauge how everyone will react to that."

"Well, as far as know, none of the other guys are gay, but I know that *I* don't care if you're gay, buddy! I doubt anyone else will care, either. And listen, I know I look kinda rough and tough, I scowl a lot, but I'm really just a big teddy bear at heart. You're safe here, man," he winks.

Rowan's kindness stirs my fragile emotional state and a surge of heat rises in my chest, catching in my throat. Tears sting the corners of my eyes as I swallow raggedly and tap a nervous rhythm on the island's granite surface with my fingernails.

"Thank you, Rowan," I say, my voice hitching and tears beginning to spill. "I—um—sorry, man!"

"Ah, buddy, come here," he says, stepping around the island and embracing me in a tight, brotherly hug. Rowan is six and a half feet tall, and I wrap my arms around his stomach, chuckling through my sobs.

"Helluva introduction, huh?" I jest. "Hi, I'm Charlie or *Charles* now, I guess. I'm a washed-up drunk clearly suffering from an identity crisis, I'm gay, and—*bonus prize*—I'm falling apart right before your eyes!"

"You remind me of my favorite cousin. He's gay, too," Rowan answers simply.

"I'm so sad, Rowan," I say, pulling back from him and wiping my eyes. "I've let myself down so many times. But—no!" I brandish my arms before me, expelling the negativity. "I'm starting over here. Everything will be okay. I'm here now, I'm alive. And that's all that matters."

"That's right."

A beat of silence rings.

"Well, anything you need to get off your chest, Rowan?" I banter, fiercely rubbing my eyes and neck.

"Actually, yes. Today is the first day I woke up feeling good, physically, you know? No headache or achy muscles, and the first thought that crossed my mind was, 'man I feel so good, I wanna get plastered!' Isn't that some *bullshit*? Finally starting to feel better, and my first instinct is to fuck it all up again," he exhales, scraping my plate into a dog's bowl and rinsing it in the sink.

"Oh, I so get that. Um, do we have a dog here?"

"Sometimes Tessa brings her therapy dog in, Reni, and he's here today. So, you're moving out here permanently, then?" he asks, drying his hands on a towel with his hip propped against the counter of the sink.

"Yeah. I decided on the plane ride out here that I'm not going back to Missouri. I can't, it's too dangerous for me. I've got to start my life over. I've got to *finally* do what I should have done over two years ago."

"I've been thinking about that, too. I'm from Indiana, and there's nothing back there for me but a trailer and a busted-ass van."

"Right? And sorry for assuming you're from California," I say, suddenly exhausted. "Oof, I'm a mess, man. I'm gonna go take a shower and see if I can pull myself together before groups start. Thanks for being cool, Rowan."

"Sure thing, bud," he says.

*****

I rest upon the fountain's ledge with one foot dangling in its cool water and one foot upon the satiny green grass. Clouds drift by lazily in the bright blue sky, the wind stirring the leaves of a colossal rosewood. Sunshine roasts my body, sweat sticky and wet on my arms and legs, and it soothes my sore muscles. In maintaining the status quo of rehab, I have lost myself in workout routines, restrictive dieting, and novel after novel. Yet another typical stay for Mr. Rehab himself.

"What's up, Charles?" Tessa beckons from the outdoor living room.

"Hey, Tessa," I answer, neither moving nor breaking my gaze from the sky.

"Enjoying the sunshine?" she asks pleasantly.

"Sweating my balls off, more like, but it feels nice after the workout I did this morning."

Tessa giggles. "You still gonna be up for walking the ponies later this evening?"

"Of course!" I say, turning my head to grin at her. "I wouldn't forsake Maverick for love nor money!"

"Y'all do have a very special bond," she agrees.

"We're gypsy wanderers. We understand one another."

"Are you a gypsy now, too?" she banters.

"Sure, why not?"

"Well, how about you bring your sweaty gypsy balls up to my office and we'll go over your discharge plan for tomorrow?" she says, then gasps and clamps her hand to her mouth. "Shit! I just heard what I said!"

I crumple from laughter, my legs curling up to my body and dripping water on my chest. "'Bring my sweaty gypsy balls to your office,' eh? Tessa, you *know* I don't swing that way!" I tease, guffawing.

"Oh, wow! Oh, my goodness! I was trying to be funny and it went horribly wrong!" she whines, blushing a deep shade of scarlet that matches her exquisite tresses.

"Oh no, no worries!" I sigh happily. *"That* was some funny shit, Tessa!"

"Thank the Lord I said it to *you* and not one of the other guys!" she gulps.

"Right? Oh, wow. Brilliant! And yeah, let me grab some water and I'll meet you up there."

Tessa nods, shaking her head in embarrassment, and ascends the wide spiral staircase to her office. I grab a bottle of water and three pickles, then dart up the stairs to her office. In the mansion's glory days, this room belonged to the live-in maid and is rather sparse and small compared to the other rooms. It has two large windows, which surround her desk and laptop, and a closet with sliding mirror doors. Her plush, cream-colored patient chair is placed in the corner, facing away from the mirrors and toward her desk and windows.

"Gotta have your pickles, huh?" she says waggishly.

"Always!" I chirp.

"Do they ever trigger you? Since you used pickle juice as a chaser so often?" she asks as I take a seat in her patient chair.

"Not at all! I would *never*! Oh, my goodness, *no*! I could *never* let vodka spoil my love of pickles. My pickles were around *way* before that wretched vodka!" I rattle emphatically, my eyes wide and serious.

"Damn, you *do* love your pickles!" Tess chortles.

"I certainly do," I retort genially.

"You know, you might try implementing some of that defense in other areas of your life," she quips, arching an eyebrow.

"You sassy therapist, you!" I exclaim in mock shock, taking a crunchy bite.

"I'm just saying," she grins.

"No, you're right, you're right."

"That's what I like to hear," she winks. "Now, let me check and see if you have any final assessments we need to do. I don't think you should, though. I believe we only have your discharge assessment to complete," she mutters, opening her laptop and typing. "Yup, just your discharge assessment. But, before we start that, let's chat a bit."

"Sure," I nod.

"How are you feeling about leaving tomorrow? Are you excited about starting IOP and sober living at Simple Recovery?"

I rub my fingers over the woven fabric of her patient chair and finish chewing my last pickle.

"I am, yes. I'm excited that I'm *actually* doing it, you know? That I'm actually following through and going to sober living *and* IOP. I know I've said that I would the whole time I've been here, but I honestly didn't *know* if I would. Because I always say a lot of horseshit throughout rehab, and most of the time I genuinely do mean it, until the last few days, when I usually decide I'm ready to drink and fuck it all up again. But, I didn't do that this time. I'm honestly kind of proud of myself! It's scary as fuck, but I *am* proud."

Tessa's hazel eyes sparkle as she smiles and shakes her head.

"What?" I ask innocently.

"I'm proud of you, too, Charles! I'm proud of you for being proud of *yourself*!"

"Awe, shucks," I say.

"No, really! That's amazing! And you *should* be proud! What you're doing is huge! You're breaking the cycle, do you see that?" she implores.

"I am, aren't I? I've finally broken the cycle of running away to rehab for a few weeks, then running back home to drink again."

"Yes! And *sure* you're scared! A part of your mind isn't used to this, it isn't used to you taking control and doing what's best for you. Oh, I'm so excited for you! I've heard great things about Simple Recovery, too, and your sober house is nicer than my damn house!" she says, slapping her thigh.

"You're shitting me! I haven't been told anything about my sober house yet. I've only been told I've been assigned to one—Viva, I think it's called?"

"Yes, Viva House. It's in Fountain Valley, very close to the coast, and it's in a *very* nice suburb."

"Oh, wow. That's not my experience with sober homes back in Missouri, but then again, this is California, a haven of recovery!" I beam. "Oh, I know it's petty and materialistic and pampered and bratty and a bunch of other privileged things, but it makes me feel so much better knowing that I'm going to a nice sober house!"

"Hey now, don't demean yourself like that! There's nothing wrong with wanting to live in a nice house. And, think about it, you were fortunate enough

THE FROG NO MORE

to be raised in a very safe, clean, and loving environment, so that's exactly what you need in order to heal. It's not that you're petty or materialistic or bratty, it's that you need comfort and respite right now. And you know who I hear talking when you call yourself all those names?"

"Who?" I reply feebly, already knowing the answer.

"Your 'dark wolf.' I hear Charles' dark wolf telling him he doesn't deserve a nice sober house because he's a piece of shit drunk and has hurt his family and friends for a decade. I hear Charles' dark wolf getting frightened that Charles is growing strong without him. I hear Charles' dark wolf resorting to his same old tricks, and they're starting to feel tired and lame, don't you think?" she says, a hint of sass and reproach to her tone.

"Yeah," I mutter reluctantly.

"I hear your dark wolf, Charles! Listen to me, because I mean this: you are *not* a failure, you are *not* unworthy because you didn't make it as an actor. You are not useless and insignificant and unimportant because you're not on the stage or in movies or on television. Are you hearing what I'm saying? Just because that dream didn't come true for you doesn't mean that you are a waste of space and life. Those thoughts are where your dark wolf lives. Those thoughts are what he feeds on. And damn it, you know how much I *mean* this!" she pleads, her eyes brimming with sincerity.

A ball of fire erupts in my throat and tears leak from my eyes. Tessa swivels her chair around the desk and rolls closer to me, clasping one of my hands in hers.

"I wish so much that you had an Oscar and were starring on Broadway, Charles! I really and truly do! I wish you could fly all over the world and immerse yourself in culture, and study art and languages. God, I *wish* that was your life right now, Charles! With my whole heart! I wish I could snap my fingers and make all that a reality for you!

"But I can't. And none of that *really matters* anyways. None of that is a testament to you or your character. None of *that* has to define you! You've got to let all that go. You've got to forgive yourself! You've got to mourn the death of your mom and your Granny Norma Jean, you've got to forgive yourself for not making it as an actor and mourn that lost dream, and you've got to work on the relationship with your dad, sister, aunt, and cousin. And, above all and most importantly, you've *got* to begin loving yourself again, the way you did when you were a young boy and in college. You've got to, or you're going to die a painful and lonely death. There's no doubt about it. And that would absolutely crush me and break my heart."

Tessa's face is a portrait of empathy, love, and concern. Her chin quivers as she holds eye contact with me and I sob, pulling my legs up to my chest and wrapping my arm around them, still clutching her hand in mine.

"You have the most beautiful and amazing light about you, Charles. Your 'light wolf' is full of vitality, full of compassion, full of acceptance, full of love. Feed him, and only him, from now on. You have the full package, silly!" she grins rosily. "You're smart, caring, and charming—use those tools to start over and build something new and beautiful. Use the pain of your past as fuel. Have you been writing?"

"I have not," I say hoarsely, sniffling and swallowing, then pull my hand from Tessa's to wipe my face and eyes. "I have not. I tried the first couple of weeks, but it was just a bunch of rambling about shame and fear, nothing coherent. But, um, thank you so much, Tessa. I have felt my dark wolf creeping back in lately, and I needed to hear all that. It's because I'm so used to operating as the dark wolf. Sometimes I feel like I'm pretending, that I'm a huge fake when I'm doing breath works and yoga. Like, I'll be right in the middle of a really good session, where I'm vibing and feeling all the right feels—I'm on the astral plane of forgiveness—and this little voice will whisper maniacally in the back of my mind, 'isn't this fun? Isn't this cute? But you know it will *never last*. You'll never actually keep up with *any* of this, and you know that, *stupid boy.*' And the most fucked up, saddest part of it all is that I *believe that voice* more than anyone or anything else in my life."

"Hmm," Tessa tilts her head. "Prove him wrong. And you're taking all the right steps to do that, you know? One day at a time. And you *are* proving him wrong—you've made excellent strides in coping with the grief of losing your mom! Did you finish your letter to her?"

"I did. Yesterday afternoon, actually. It turned out to be much longer than I anticipated, but once I started writing, it just sorta poured out of me. I felt like I could hear her answers to some of the questions I was asking, too. Not like an actual whisper or anything like that, which would have been spooky and fun, but more like I knew the answers to the questions I was asking. And my mom always gave extremely direct and comforting answers."

Sunlight trickles through the windows as the sun moves in the sky, brightening the room.

"Did you write to her about your dad?" Tessa asks tentatively.

"I did," I nod thoughtfully, biting my lower lip. "Extensively. I mean, it's important to know I rarely blamed my dad for anything that happened in my childhood. I always felt like he was doing the best he could, and was just as heartbroken as the rest of us. That was never an issue for me. And even when I *would* get mad about the stepmoms, I never hated him, even though I told him that, and did some very malicious things to him. I regret that now, *especially* a few choice words I said to him after Mom died. But, I was young and in pain, so I went for the jugular. I learned in that moment, though, because going for the jugular isn't actually satisfying. As soon as the words fell from my mouth I wanted to reel them back in. I don't think I have a propensity for cruelty. It feels unnatural to me, yet I am so cruel when I'm drunk. And I think I know why, but back to the point. I asked my mom if she thought Dad and I could move on from all the tragedy and heartache we have experienced. Not that we forget it, but that we recognize we were both broken people stumbling through the world. I asked her if she thought we could somehow find our way back to one another and repair the damage."

"And what did she say?" she asks softly.

"She said yes, but I was also reminded of something Granny Norma Jean, his mom, once told me. She said a relationship was like a crystal glass, and the worst thing you could do to someone you love was to hurt them or lie to them, and if you did that, it was like shattering the glass. Sure, the pieces could be put back together, but it would never be the same. That's how I feel about my dad. We can repair the damage, but I don't think we'll ever be the same again, you know? I've grown too old, and too much has happened. There will always be great love and respect between us, but it will never be the same. Anyways, as long as I keep doing what I should be doing, we will ultimately find peace with one another. It was a very reassuring moment, writing that letter to her—it was a *beautiful* moment. I was up in the yoga loft, looking out over the valley and sky, writing and listening for her answers. It gave me hope and motivation for the future."

"Wonderful!" she grins, leaning back in her chair. "Cherish these moments! You'll have many more to come, too, the longer you maintain your sobriety. And how are you coming along with detailing and understanding *your* role in perpetuating your alcoholic cycle?"

"Whoa, subject change!" I giggle, feigning whiplash.

"Gotta keep you on your toes!" she snaps her fingers. "And we're also covering the majority of your discharge assessment, two birds with one stone."

"Ah, Tessa, those poor birds," I smirk. "But, efficient as always. You're truly one of my favorite therapists, you know that? I have enjoyed our sessions so much! And they've been so often and *long*, compared to my other treatment centers! I mean, you dug deep! And I thank you for it!"

Tessa fans her face. "That is all the reward I need for doing this job! But you're not buttering me up that easily!" she wags her finger at me.

"Dang it!" I laugh. "Ah, well. Can't blame me for trying. I *have* accepted my role in it all, though. I've accepted my fascination with a maudlin, tortured existence. I've separated myself from myself, so to speak, objectively, and analyzed my life. Which I had done before, but I'd never done it with the acceptance that *I'm* the driving force behind all of this. I had to come to terms with the fact that I love being drunk, I love inflicting chaos on myself, and I love feeling victimized. I couldn't see it all—the big picture—until recently. I can see that I was so full of anger during my first dozen rounds of detoxes and rehabs because I didn't want to confront my trauma. I was fighting it tooth and nail. And now, I realize that by continuously running to rehabs, I have allowed myself to grow complaisant. I have been happily lost in a cycle for the last couple of years. I have prolonged my alcoholism in this way because I have been scared to get sober and put myself out there. I've been afraid to *try*. And I mean *really* put myself out there, really *try* something again, without worrying about the fear of failing. I failed so hard at acting, and I've spent *years* punishing myself. But, I also *enjoyed* the punishment. I catered to myself and placated myself, you know? I have to admit that, I have to own that. I have to admit these things about myself, admit their power, so that I can move on from it all. And it's fucking exhausting, Tessa! Shit!" I declare.

"Sure it is! But it's the work we *must* do if we want to continue to evolve and prosper. And it's wonderful that you're admitting your character defects to yourself. Truly, Charles, those are quite remarkable discoveries you've made about yourself. Refrain from judgment and shame, though. I have made a note in your file for your future therapist that you have a tendency to demean and discredit yourself. You've got to keep working on that, Charles. Most of IOP will be material you've heard dozens of times, but that doesn't mean the work you're doing on yourself can stop. You've got to take time and focus on healing yourself. And I say this in seriousness—*take your time*. You know, at Viva House you're not required to start looking for a job until you've been there for ninety days. They very much support the idea of continuing your therapy after rehab. Take advantage of this time, Charles! Write your book! You never know, it might help you heal."

"What? That's nuts! *Ninety days*? I mean, it's friggin' amazing, but nuts! What are we supposed to do for money and food, and stuff like that?" I balk.

"Everything will be taken care of for you. This is yet another stellar opportunity laid at your feet, Charles. Don't *squander* this one," she warns.

"You're right, Tessa. And believe me, I realize how lucky I am. I mean, people just don't get this many chances, you know? And I can only tempt fate so many times before I wear out my welcome."

"Gratitude, Charles. Let gratitude guide you. And I *know* that won't be hard for you unless *you* want it to be," she chides lovingly.

"Oh, Tessa. Is this my time? Am I ready?" I ask wearily.

"Only you can answer that, Charles. But, you are in the perfect position to be ready."

"Yes," I sigh. "A familiar position, honestly. But this time, I shall refrain from shooting it in the face. At least I hope so."

"Don't give up on yourself, no matter what you do. You can be your loudest critic or your loudest cheerleader. And, between us, I believe you're gonna make it, and one day your story is going to change lives."

"One can only hope, Tessa."

"And hope and hope and hope," she nods.

*****

The hills of Yorba Linda disappear, gobbled up by strip malls and drab buildings as I ride in Affinity's van to Simple Recovery. I am its lone passenger, occupying the middle seat in the first of three rows. My driver wears a green baseball cap covering his short brown hair and bops his head to the music playing on the radio, his window partially rolled down.

"You from California? Or did you come out here for recovery?" he asks, making eye contact with me in the rearview mirror. He has dark brown eyes and bushy eyebrows. I would place his age around twenty-five or twenty-six.

"Well, you know, I guess I *have* moved out here now. Wow, I don't think it hit me until now," I chuckle. "And I'm from Missouri, the Kansas City area."

"Kansas City Chiefs!" he thunders, cackling.

"Oh? You a fan of the Chiefs?"

"Oh yeah! I'm originally from Iowa, but my mom's side is all from Kansas City, and my family used to take trips there a lot when I was growing up."

"Right on! My Aunt Trella is a massive fan," I nod.

"So, you decided to stay in California, huh? That's awesome, bud!" he smiles.

"Thanks. I knew if I went back to Kansas City I stood no chance of staying sober. Hell, I probably would have relapsed on the flight back, knowing me. So, I finally decided to do the whole shebang. I'll be in an intensive outpatient program for three or four months, then OP, sober living for at least a year, and lots of meetings. I'm willing to get a Sponsor and work The Steps. I'm so fucking tired of being a drunk, I'll do whatever it takes," I groan.

"Listen, bud, that's perfect! You're exactly where you need to be—and lean into it, dude! I did all that, too, and I'm still in sober living."

"How long have you been sober?" I ask.

"I have one year, eight months, and thirteen days clean," he answers proudly.

"Holy shit! That's so much time! That's awesome!"

"Thank you, bud! But it all started right where you're at now, going to a sober house. I don't know much about Viva, but I know it's nice, and Simple takes very good care of its patients. Hang in there, man, it gets better."

I shake my head in agreement, a thin mist of tears clouding my eyes, and glance at the floorboard.

"Yup. One day at a time," I say quietly.

10

Klaus the Savior

August 2021
Clinton, Missouri
35 Years Old

Dusty golden meadows of my boyhood whiz by, memories bubbling forth as I drive Esteban down Highway 7. I tighten my grip on the steering wheel, smiling, and flick cigarette ashes out the cracked window.

"A little over one year sober, my first book published, and my first podcast recorded!" I grin. "I *finally* feel like I'm trying!"

Anticipating the curve, I release my foot from the gas pedal and allow my mind to drift. These are the same fields I played in as a kid, revving my red Kawasaki four-wheeler up and down gravel roads and Highway 7, pretending to run from the law or "bad guys." Oh, the innocence of youth, for I also fractured my neck and received my first DUI on this highway. What would I say to that little boy now, were I to stumble across him?

"That you're in for a helluva ride," I chuckle. "A *helluva* ride. But somehow, I think he already knew that."

Taking a left on U Highway, I drive a mile, then turn into an old dirt driveway. Killing the engine, I lean back in my seat, surveying the land before me. Robust oak, walnut, and elm trees sway in the summer's breeze beneath a clear blue sky. A sparkling pond gleams a few feet from the worn dirt road, placid and inviting in this heat. I sigh, remembering a winter long ago, my dad hoisting my body up and down by my armpits as my galoshes busted through the ice. We giggled the whole time, covered in snow and eager to provide water for our thirsty cows, horses, and mules.

"Our pond," I breathe. "But not anymore."

Pushing down my despair, I open Esteban's door and walk to the rusted metal gate, placing my hands gently on its rails. The faint chattering of birds soothes me, and I take a deep breath, relishing the earthy scents of the fields, familiar and calming. Closing my eyes, I see my younger self tearing across this meadow, laughing merrily with Granny Norma Jean and Brod as we make our way toward the abandoned and dilapidated stone house. In my mind's eye, Brod streaks by in a blur of curly white-blonde hair, shrieking with giggles and chased by Coffee, Granny Norma Jean's small, white and brown beagle; I dance, goofy and with glee, on the back of Grandpa John's massive green Polaris four-wheeler, striking poses and snacking on a dill pickle.

Tears sting the corners of my eyes and a hot lump clogs my throat. Opening them, I swallow dryly and take a ragged breath.

"One day I will buy you back," I vow, scanning the pastures and tree line. "I *promise* I'll get you back, build a glorious home on you, and take care of you forever and ever." My voice hitches and I stare up at the cloudless sky, collecting myself. "I promise, Grandpa John. I promise."

Moonlight pools on the linoleum of my kitchen floor, a cricket chirping loudly from outside the window. Cradling Klaus in my arms, I rub his furry neck, burying my face in his side.

"I love you so much, buddy!" I whisper, showering him with kisses and smelling his warm, clean scent. "But I think your dad is on the brink of an emotional breakdown, and I'm not sure why."

He cranes his neck up at me, his chartreuse eyes locking with mine, and slowly blinks.

"Awe, buddy, the slow blink. I love you, too," I say, scratching the top of his head. "I love you, too. You know what? You've never seen your dad drunk, you know that? Isn't that *amazing*? If you only knew, bud. If you only knew."

Petting the bottom of his chin, I pace our apartment floor, searching for the root of my irksome anxiety. Stopping to pinch the carpet between my toes, I release Klaus from my arms and sprawl upon my purple living room rug. The air is still, the space calm and quiet, yet my heart hammers in my chest. Taking a breath, I rest my eyes and stretch my arms.

"Mom?" I croak softly, hearing only my cricket friend. "Were you scared, too? When you were my age? Did you feel lost, too? 'Course, you had two children and were running a resort when you were my age. You probably had no time to feel lost, but maybe you did? I don't know. I wish you were here."

Klaus sniffs my ear loudly, then licks the side of my face affectionately. I scoop him into my arms and plop him on my chest, where he begins to groom his front paws.

"You know, I think it's this irksome feeling of wanting to accomplish a decade's worth of work in a couple of years. Which is preposterous and absurd, but then again, so am I, buddy. And I can't help the way I feel. But, I can help the way I think."

Klaus cocks his head at me as if agreeing before leaping off my chest. I rise to a sitting position and pop my back, moaning in satisfaction.

"Yes, I can most certainly help the way I think. And what I think is this, Klaus: I have every reason to be proud of myself and satisfied. I am doing the best I can, working at building a better life, and just because it's not happening overnight doesn't mean I'm doing it wrong, or I'm not worthy.

"And also—that's a super fucked up idea in the first place, don't you think? I mean, who the hell came up with 'overnight success?' It's a toxic idea!" I holler, panting slightly.

"No, anger isn't the answer, Charlie. By now, you *at least* know that." I say, shifting from the ground to my orange chair. "No, it's still a matter of taking it day by day, doing the best work you can, and finding gratitude in the small moments. That's not a bunch of horseshit, it's certainly possible if you want it to be. And I *do* want it to be," I nod, absentmindedly grasping Klaus' tail as he grazes my calf. "You're a very good listener, Klaus, you know that, babe? And one day, I'll build you tunnels and mazes in our glorious house.

"You know that's my *real* goal, right? That's what really matters to me. Building myself a safe, beautiful house to live in. Where I can write my books. *That's* the dream. *That's* the goal. And we'll get there when we're supposed to, but hopefully, that's sooner rather than later."

*****

My phone vibrates noisily from the couch cushion and I glance over, smiling at a FaceTime from Rowan, a friend of mine from Affinity Recovery in California. Anxiously plucking it from the cushion, I swipe open his call.

"Hi, Rowan!" I say, my smile evaporating as I see his face.

It has been nearly two years since I last laid eyes upon Rowan, and he looks frightfully gruff. His eyes are sunken with dark black circles, his cheeks gaunt and pale, and he's buzzed his gorgeous thick and curly auburn hair.

"Hey, buddy, what's up?" he asks shyly, a lit cigarette tucked between his lips.

"Oh, not much. Just sitting here watching *The Originals*, what're you up to?"

"Still watching your vampire shows, huh?" he chortles.

"Always," I grin.

"Right on. I'm not up to much. Sitting on the side of the street, chain-smoking cigarettes, and trying to sort out my life. And, well, I can't believe I'm actually saying this, but I'm really thinking about calling a rehab since all I've done lately is drink vodka and bang dope," he laughs bitterly.

"Oh, Rowan, I'm so sorry to hear that! Damn, that's *so not* what I expected when I saw your FaceTime, but it's okay, it's alright! You're banging dope? That's rare for you. Meth or heroin?"

"Meth. I've managed to stay away from heroin, but I've been drinking vodka and banging a lot of meth."

"Ah, man! Well, you seem sober *now*," I observe.

"I'm coming down, and I've been drinking, but I'm fairly sober, all things considered," he groans.

"Well, damn it! What happened? I thought you were in sober living in Huntington Beach and working for an art dealer!"

"Oh, I was. Until I wasn't," he says simply.

"Dude, I fucking *get that*. But what happened?"

"To be honest, I really don't know. I mean, do you ever feel like some of us aren't meant to stay sober? Like some people just can't do it? Like physically *can't*—like once they've started drinking or using, they'll never be able to stop?" he asks, a bit breathless.

"You mean some people inherently can't stay sober? No matter what? Like it's beyond them in a way?"

"Yes! Like it's impossible!" he agonizes.

"Hmm," I swallow. "I don't think anything is impossible, bud. What do you mean, though? What are you getting at? Do you think you're incapable of staying sober?"

"Yes, I think I am incapable of staying sober," he repeats confidently.

"Why do you think that?"

"Because nothing works! I've tried *everything*, and nothing works!" he cries, flustered and exasperated.

"Well, you've called the right person, then," I say, standing from my couch and searching for my pack of cigarettes. "Because I know *exactly* how you feel. For years, I didn't think it was possible for me to stay sober, either, but I celebrated a year last month, so I guess it *is*."

"Charles, that's amazing! How have you stayed sober? AA?"

"No, I haven't been to a meeting since before my last drink. Don't get me wrong, I definitely learned a shit ton from Alcoholics Anonymous *and* Narcotics Anonymous, but it wasn't going to meetings that kept me sober. Let me be clear: I used many of their principles, although not in the traditional ways. And I think you just asked the most important question—how did I *stay* sober—not how did I *get* sober? Because getting sober isn't the toughest part, and most of us rehab junkies come to that conclusion after a while. It's *staying* sober that's hard. But, let's get back to the idea that some people are incapable of staying sober. What makes you feel this way?"

"I just told you! I've tried *everything*! Rehab, IOP, sober living, jail, work release, probation, Naltrexone and Campral, going to church, painting, wellness retreats, yoga, and meditation. Do you know what's wild? I've even tried holding a fucking seance and asking my great granny, who basically raised me until she passed away when I was eleven, to haunt me anytime I try drinking or using!" he moans.

"Wow, that is some serious commitment, dude. *I* haven't even tried the seance," I jest.

"Shut up," he smiles gently. "But seriously, Charles, how have you stayed sober? Kellan said writing helped you, and I thought getting back into painting was gonna save me, but I was clearly wrong about that, too."

"Not to veer away from you, bud, but have you seen Kellan lately? I haven't heard from him in a couple of months, which is longer than usual. This is actually kinda surreal, because Kellan and I are usually talking about you and how you're doing, and now the situation is switched."

Rowan bites his bottom lip and looks away from his phone.

"Oh no, has something bad happened?" I ask, my blood turning cold.

"I bought from him," he answers quietly.

"Ah, man," I sigh. "Shit, I thought you were gonna tell me he had died or something! That's so much better than what I *thought* you were going to say."

"Yeah, that's true," he replies, crestfallen.

"But, oh well, bud! It doesn't have to be a big deal unless you make it a big deal. At least you're both still alive! And you know what? I'm beginning to think that there's no trick to staying sober other than genuinely *wanting* to stay sober. I had to *want* to take a hard look at myself, at who I had become, at what I had done with my life. I had to *want* to take ownership of my mistakes and admit my shortcomings and faults. I had to tell myself that *I* had done all of this, no one had made me do it. No one had forced me to live like a belligerent alcoholic. No one made me squander my twenties. *I* did that. And I had to admit that on some level, I liked it—shit, there I go, spouting bullshit—I *loved* it! I didn't love hurting my family and friends or putting myself in risky and embarrassing situations, but I fucking *loved* being drunk, I loved the drama of it all, and I loved the chaos. I placated myself with my own insanity. I had to admit that there were parts of being an alcoholic that I loved—I loved it because it was the only part of my life I could control at the time—and I had to be okay with that. I had to be okay with my character defects and my actions, or I was never going to be able to forgive myself for them. And I had to understand myself more completely.

"Once I was able to swallow my fear and pride, I started to work on myself in a way I'd never done before. I started to treat myself with dignity and respect. I started to treat myself the way I treat other people. I started to understand that when I was out there in my active addiction, I was doing the best that I could. I was coping as best as I knew how. I wasn't waking up each day with the intention of ruining myself and my relationships. I was waking up each day trying to survive! I was just going about it all wrong. And that's no reason to punish ourselves, you know? We don't intentionally fuck up our lives—it's the complete opposite! We try our hardest to cope and wade through life, we just have the shittiest of tools!

"And after seeing it that way, I began to forgive myself, and from there, it all sort of fell in line. It helped me start living in a much more positive way, too, because I knew that I was *finally* being true to myself. By recognizing I had been doing the best I could during my active addiction, and by taking genuine ownership of all that had happened, I was being honest and fair with myself, which is true to who I am at my core. Being true to *myself* is so important for me—I've always wanted to live a life where I'm true to myself. I know if I'm living that way, my life will have meaning and purpose, and that fulfills me. It's all very circular, really.

"Now, I'm not going to lie to you, though, and make it sound like it was all rainbows and fucking butterflies. Because it wasn't. And it sure wasn't easy, but I'll tell you one thing, it was a lot easier than figuring out how to bail myself out of jail while also battling a brutal hangover, or finding a rehab or detox so that I didn't lose my job because I'd been calling in for days, or faking a seizure so I could get a hospital bed, or telling my family, 'no, I haven't been sober for the last ten months, I've been lying to you and guzzling vodka behind your back'—you know the bullshit life. It's much easier than *that* life, and so much more rewarding.

"Listen, I know it's not the answer you probably want to hear, and I hope I didn't sound preachy or anything like that because I fucking *hate* when people get like that—all high and mighty because they've overcome something. It's like, yeah, you overcame something, that's great, but now you're an even *bigger* ass and have even *more* to overcome! But I digress."

"Yes, you do, but you always do that," he mutters with a small smile. "And you didn't get preachy. You said exactly what I needed to hear."

"Shucks, I was hoping so! But do you know what I mean, though?"

"I do, bud, I do!" he chuckles.

"Thank you," I say, mollified. "Anyways, I get where you're at, buddy, because I wanted to be ready for so many years, and there were so many times when I *really* thought I was, but then I'd end up drunk again in a matter of days. So, obviously, I wasn't ready to get sober.

"I think you have to be able to fully commit to it, you have to want it more than anything else, you have to put it above anything else, and then you can stay sober. I had to truly want to stop drinking. I had to truly want to change my life. Because once you truly want to change your life, nothing, and I mean *absolutely nothing*, can stand in your way.

"But you can't know what you don't know, you know?" I snicker. "I mean, there's no way I could have known all of this during those years of running around and trying to get—let alone stay—sober. I just wasn't ready. I thought I was—*all the time* I thought I was! But I wasn't ready to fully tackle my trauma and shortcomings until July of 2020. And it wasn't until I had been sober for *a while* that I was able to recognize all this, bud. It wasn't until I'd been sober for a few months that I finally understood despite going to all those rehabs and detoxes and psych wards, I just wasn't ready to quit drinking, or I would have quit drinking. I know it sounds so simple, but it's so true, dude. It's *so* fucking true. In my extensive experience, at least."

Rowan exhales loudly, nodding, and scratches his ear. "How did you know you were ready, though?"

"I didn't. It wasn't until I'd been sober for about six months that it finally hit me: I didn't want vodka anymore. I had never felt that before, you know? Not *once* in my life had my brain told me it no longer wanted vodka. Like, what the hell? But it was true, and the thought was absolute. I didn't want to drink vodka anymore, because I didn't want the aches and pains that go with it, and I really wanted to explore some other avenues of life. Maybe I finally got bored with vodka? I dunno, I just knew I wanted to take my life in a different direction, and that direction didn't include vodka."

"Ah fuck, you're right, dude. I just have to decide that I want to do something different with my life, and fucking *do it* already!" he says dourly, clenching his jaw.

"Hey, but for whatever reason, that's so much easier said than done! It's not as simple as it sounds," I retort. "It's like we have to get some foreign part of our brain on board, too, you know? I know it sounds extreme, but it was almost like an unknown, subconscious part of me had to authorize the change before it could happen. I *swear* it's not a choice—it's *much* deeper than that! For me, at least. It's like there had to be a change on my cellular level before I could stay sober, which sounds super dramatic, but it's the only way I can describe it," I grin.

"You know," Rowan says, rubbing his chin and crinkling his eyebrows. "I've never thought of that before, but that's a good point, man. Like, it's a *really* good point. I mean, I know I want to be sober, *I know it in my heart*, but for whatever reason, I can't seem to *stay* sober."

"Listen, I've said that exact same sentence a thousand times. A thousand damn times!"

"But look at you now!"

"Far better than the life I used to be living," I agree. "It's really nice to be proud of myself again. I mean, I've still got my problem areas, for sure, but I love myself again. I love what I'm doing, and after over a decade of hating what I was doing, it's a beautiful change."

"Oh, dude, I have no idea what that feels like. I don't think I've been proud of myself since elementary school," he chuckles hollowly. "Seriously."

"I feel that. But, believe me, it doesn't have to stay that way. And I used to fucking hate when people would say shit like that! Hate it! But it's also so true," I shrug. "So, now I understand why people said that, and I also understand why I reacted the way I did when they said it. It was such a moment, realizing all of that."

"Oh, Charles and his 'moments!'" he teases.

"Shut up," I banter playfully.

"Nah, man, I'm happy you're still having them. I could use a few of them myself right now," he sighs dejectedly and leans against a stucco wall.

"So, where are you now? Do you have a place to live?"

"It's rough right now, Charles, I'm not going to lie. I've spent a few nights on the streets, crashed at some trap houses, and spent some time with an old friend of mine, in his basement. He came out here a couple of years before me, and we reconnected in sobriety, but we've both relapsed since then. He's actually a good guy, just super into drugs, and I can't hang around him that long without feeling terrible. I remember how we would play together, as kids. Innocent. And then I look around at what we've become, and it's too much, it overwhelms me. So, I drink."

"Ah, bud. I *so* understand where you're at right now. I hate this for you, Rowan. Are you eating at all?"

His eyes fill with tears and he gasps.

"No, Charles, things are really, really bad right now. Really bad, man," he sobs, covering his face with his hand. "I've lost all my friends here because I've relapsed. Well, I haven't lost them, but it's not like they can hang out with me now that I'm a walking shit show. I *never* should have stayed! I should have gone back home to Indiana, but I'm a dumbass and stayed here. I barely have any money left, I don't know what I'm going to do for food or booze or drugs, and then I'll start detoxing. Fuck! And I'm not saying all this to be, like, sorry for myself. I'm *not* sorry for myself, I know *I'm* the piece of shit that did this. I just hate myself right now and I don't know what to do, man. I don't know what the fuck to do! And I'm so angry at myself! Like, *really*, Rowan? Rehab? *Again*? Really? You stupid piece of shit rat bastard!"

"Oh, Rowan," I whisper, my chin trembling. "Hey, buddy, listen to me, alright? I love you very much, okay? I mean it. I love you very much! And it's okay if things are really bad right now. It's okay. You *didn't do this on purpose*—even if it feels like it—you didn't! Okay? Don't kick your own ass over something you didn't mean to do, you hear? Take a deep breath for me, close your eyes, count to four, exhale, and then let's figure out a plan, alright? You up to that? Give me the street you're on and I'll start pulling up hospitals and detoxes in your area. We're fucking pros at this, dude. Where you wanna go? Mr. Rehab will get you in the finest one there is, best believe that!" I whoop goofily.

Rowan guffaws through his tears, wipes his eyes, and inhales loudly through his nose.

"That's no shit! You'll have me in the friggin' Ritz of rehabs in no time," he giggles.

"I'll for sure do my best! And you know my spiel on rehab—you may not leave those doors and stay sober for the rest of your life, but you sure can learn a lot about yourself and do some great work. I discovered so much about myself during rehab, and grew so much from my experiences, I most definitely would not be the man I am today were it not for rehabs, detoxes, and psych wards. They made me a better man.

"And I know that can happen for you, too, bud. I know it! You worked so hard while we were at Affinity. I never told you that enough, and I should have, and I'm sorry for that. I should have told you much more often that I saw how hard you were working. I saw you reading 'The Big Book' and 'The Basic Text' each evening. I saw you taking notes, constantly revising your Relapse Prevention Plan, and doing breathwork on your own. I saw a desire to stay clean and sober in you, Rowan, and now it's time for you to see it in yourself. And lemme tell ya, it's a magical fucking time, dude! I'm so excited for you to have *your* moments. And I'm so excited to see what you do with all your amazing gifts, and the imprint you leave on this world. You're an inspiring man, Rowan, and I deeply value our friendship."

"Damn, Charles, thank you so much. Sometimes I just need to hear someone cares, you know? I just need to know at least *one* person cares that I'm trying. And I love you, too, buddy. So much! I mean, damn! 'Bout to make me go gay for you over here, talking so nice and sweet to me."

"Rowan, holy hell!" I chuckle loudly. "Oh, that's funny. And this isn't the end, buddy. It's just another beginning," I smile.

*****

Klaus gingerly crawls onto my lap, offering a slow blink of love. Gently scratching his head and ears, I blink slowly in return.

"What's up, my best buddy?" I murmur. "What're you doing?"

He presses his head against my hand, sniffs my knuckles, and licks my palm and fingers.

"Oh, Klaus the Savior, I love you so much," I chuckle, rubbing between his shoulder blades.

His intelligent and understanding chartreuse eyes, lined with luxurious black fur, sweep over me before closing for a nap. I stare at him, dumbfounded with love, and wonder if he is responsible for the majority of my spiritual awakening.

"Are you my kitty healer? My kitty Buddha?" I chortle tenderly and chew my bottom lip, ponderance overtaking me. "But really, what *is* 'god,' Klaus? I've battled with this question for over two decades. Is it Jesus or Allah or Zeus? Or is it Ra or Shiva or Odin or Ganesha or Diana or Quetzalcoatl? Those are all I can think of right now, but I know there's *lots* more."

A beat of silence rings through our apartment.

"Why are we so fascinated with the concept of 'god?' And why am I *not*? Why am I so indifferent to religion? Or maybe I only *think* I am? I do wonder about it an awful lot to say I'm indifferent, huh?"

Klaus breathes deeply, ignoring every word I say, or so it seems, and I sigh, resting my head on the couch.

Religion began to shimmer in my peripheral a few months ago, and I find myself thoroughly confused regarding its origin and motive, for I've never experienced intimacy with religion. I've attended several places of worship, and read bits of various religious texts (strangely, I've read more of The Book of Mormon than anything else) but I've never formed a relationship or reliance on any one religion. I've never felt a kindred connection with religion. I've also never felt the need or desire to deny religion or embrace philosophical arguments that reject its teachings and influence. No, I find myself rather indifferent and ambivalent regarding religion.

However, I do have my beliefs. I live my life by a set of beliefs I've spent years cultivating.

I firmly believe there is a force that exists beyond what I am capable of perceiving. I firmly believe in a force greater than myself, and it is this force that I have turned my life over to. This vague, obscure notion of a universal system of balance and accountability is where I have found my spiritual awakening.

I believe we have the power to be benevolent and empathetic, just as I believe we have the power to be malevolent and apathetic. And I firmly believe this is measured. It is witnessed, absorbed, evaluated, retained, and justly appointed. I firmly believe if I want to live a beautiful, meaningful life, it is incumbent upon me to operate from the core of who I am: one who values love, acceptance, and compassion above all else. This does not mean I am without flaw, because, well, *clearly*—take a gander at my life! But I strive to release love and compassion into the universe, for at the end of the day, it is all that matters to me. To send love and encouragement into the universe.

"Oh, Klaus," I fawn. "You grounded me. You stabilized me, and I've finally been able to figure out a few questions that have plagued me for years. You little goober, you!"

He yawns and runs his sandpaper tongue across my hand. I slide onto my back, careful to keep him on my chest, and unfurl my legs.

"C'mon, let's take a little nap," I mumble drowsily. "Maybe our dreams hold the answers to all of our questions."

11

Wenches & Trollops Take Europe

July 2022
Zürich/Wengen, Switzerland
Paris, France
36 Years Old

"What's the plan, Lassie?" I ask, standing with a stretch to disembark the plane.

"Well, we should probably drop off our bags at Bert's house real quick. He sent the code to the group text and said he left the key under his doormat. Then I thought we could grab some food and explore the city? Bert has class until three, and Sawyer's flight gets in at four, in a few hours," she answers, slinging her hefty backpack over her shoulder.

"Perf! You're so smart, you've got it all planned out! Is Sawyer meeting us at Bert's later this afternoon?"

"Yup!"

"Wow, she's very travel savvy, doing this all on her own!" I marvel, referring to Anne's younger sister, Sawyer.

"She really is," Anne nods.

We plod our way through the exit of the Zürich airport and I hop through the sliding glass doors.

"Finally, a cigarette!" I cry with glee, rummaging through my backpack.

"Did the nicotine patches help?" Anne asks sympathetically.

"You know, they really did, actually! But there's nothing like smoking an *actual* cigarette, you know?" I exhale, satiated.

"But you're seriously quitting next year?" Anne gapes.

"Yup, I'm really gonna do it! I mean, I have to. I've smoked for so long, it's so bad for me, and they're so damn expensive. Besides, I gave up my beloved vodka, so I figure cigarettes shan't be too terribly difficult," I shrug.

"That's a good point, Lassie," Anne smiles, as bewitchingly beautiful as ever, her shiny black hair in an adorable and messy bun.

We stand on the street curb of the airport while Anne coordinates an Uber.

"Anywhere, in particular, you'd like to go first?" she says, tapping her phone.

"The Grossmünster, for sure," I answer immediately. "I've thought about using it as a setting for a novel, and I'd really like to get the full scope of it, inside and out."

"The Grossmünster!" Anne giggles. "Oh, that's so fun! I think I had that on the travel doc?"

"You did!" I chirp. "Also, your Google travel document was epic, Lassie! I mean, I wasn't surprised, because I know you, but wow! C'est magnifique!" I kiss my fingertips.

"Thank you!" she beams. "Alright, our Uber should be here in five minutes."

I gaze at the magnificent twin towers of the Grossmünster, reaching elegantly to the heavens above, adorned with detailed statues on the exterior walls, and row after row of perfectly arched windows. Stepping back for a better view, I grin at Anne.

"Do you want to go up one of the towers?" she asks.

"Yes!" I clap my hands together. "I didn't realize we could do that, how fun!"

"Yup," she whips out her phone and pulls up the travel doc. "It says here that we're able to climb up the Karlsturm Tower—oh, shit, it's one hundred and eighty-seven stairs, but that's okay because the views are supposed to be the best in the city!"

"Oh yeah, I knew I'd be walking and climbing on this trip. No worries,

I came to explore! Take us to the Karlsturm Tower, Lassie!" I declare triumphantly.

Anne leads the way, handling the exchange of foreign currency, and we find ourselves opening an ancient wooden door to reveal a stone spiral staircase.

"Oh, wow," I breathe, "this is legit old!"

Anne giggles and begins to ascend the stairs. I fall in step behind her, my hand hovering over the timeworn walls. It is a tight squeeze, and my legs tingle with heat the further we climb.

"I wonder if it's like this the whole way up?" I say, growing short of breath.

"Kinda makes you dizzy, huh?" Anne chortles.

"A little," I agree.

"Oh, wait—oh, Lassie!" she whispers joyfully.

I glance up, realizing the spiral staircase has brought us to an open level of the tower, with wide wooden beams serving as the floor, walls, and ceiling. The thick smell of warm wood lingers, and a tiny, arched window offers a framed view of Zürich.

"Wow!" I gush, noticing a wooden staircase leading to a level above. "I guess the spiral staircase part is over, and now maybe it's a series of these wooden floors?"

Creaking up the wooden stairs, we conquer several similar floors, huffing and puffing from the exertion, until we emerge at the top level. It is in the shape of a hexagon, with each wall containing a large, glassless window offering a sweeping, panoramic view of the entire city of Zürich. A cool breeze flows through the windows, a welcome relief after the stuffy climb. Anne sits on a metal bench in the center and sighs languidly.

"Well, it's *definitely* worth the climb," I muse.

"Oh, most certainly, Lassie. I'm gonna sit here and rest a spell before taking some pictures."

"Excellent idea, Lassie."

I take a seat beside her and stare at the Limmat River. We are silent for a moment, relishing the beauty of Zürich.

"Shall we float the Limmat after this? Gather our energy perhaps?" I suggest.

"Oh, Lassie, *that's* an excellent idea. Oh, this is just everything right now,"

Anne coos, "but yes, my energy is waning. I tell you, Lassie, I needs must get thyself to a nunnery, and soon, for I've lost my mind quite completely."

I erupt in a riot of laughter and pat her back. "Oh, Las, never fear. I lost my mind hours ago, and I've been prattling to myself like a madman while we've walked around Zürich. It's just 'cause we haven't slept. We're becoming delirious."

"How delicious," Anne mutters, her British lilt surfacing.

"How scrumptious," I agree, matching her affected accent.

"Shall we wait a moment before our float, though? Bert should be done with class soon, and I think he's going to meet us here, that way he can float with us," she says, rising from the bench and pulling out her phone.

"Oh, happy lovely, yes."

"Wonderful. I shall snap a few photos, then take a little nappy nap on the church pews downstairs until he arrives. But first, I have a question I'd like to ask you, Lassie. And I don't mean to upset you, I just thought we should talk about it before the trip gets going."

"Sure, what's that?"

"I talked to Bert and Sawyer last week, and we all agreed that we should ask you a question: if we were to have a glass of wine with dinner, would that be a trigger for you? And if it is, which of course we completely understand, then we will happily refrain. We're all so proud of how far you've come in your sobriety, and I don't want to do *anything* to jeopardize that—and neither do Bert or Sawyer."

"Oh, Lassie, y'all *really are* the *best* of the best, you know that? Thank you so much for caring about me like that! I love you all so much for it. And I have no issues with y'all having some wine at dinner or whenever you want. Believe me, alcohol has most definitely lost its appeal for me."

"He no longer dances the sexy dance for you, eh?" she winks.

"You know, come to think of it, he never was that sexy of a dancer. He was actually a terrible, *terrible* dancer."

"He really was, wasn't he?" she concurs.

"The worst."

Anne knocks her shoulder against mine, and I lay back on the metal bench,

THE FROG NO MORE

perfectly at peace with life in this peacefully perfect moment.

Rounding the corner of Bert's living room, I find him lounging on an *L*-shaped couch with his laptop, the windows of his second-story apartment open to the streets below, and the hubbub of Zürich nightlife trickling in.

"I'm so happy you're here," he says sincerely, standing from the couch and embracing me in a hug.

"I'm so happy I'm here, too," I reply earnestly, squeezing him tightly. "I've missed you all these years!"

"I've missed you, too!" he murmurs, swaying from side to side as he continues our hug.

After a moment, we pull apart and I look him over. No matter how much older we get, Bert ceases to age: tall and lanky, although sporting a bit more muscle than in our youth, and boyishly handsome. He wears his light blond hair short, and intelligent glasses cover his piercing blue eyes.

"You've packed on some muscle, eh?"

"A little," he answers shyly, resuming his place on the couch.

"Right on! Life in Switzerland is treating you well, then?"

"It is! How's life back in good ol' Missouri?"

I plop onto the couch near him, facing the windows.

"You know, I love it. I have a much simpler life than I ever anticipated, but I really do love it."

"I don't know if I'd call writing book after book simple," he retorts playfully.

"Yeah, that does keep things interesting," I agree.

"I *loved* your first one, bud. It was so good and *so* brave. I was really proud of you! Parts of it were hard to read, but just because I didn't know how bad it got for you. I mean, I knew some of it, and I knew it was rough for you, but you *really* went through it!"

"I fucking did, bud. I fucking did. But you know, I wouldn't change a bit of it now. Isn't that wild? But I wouldn't. Because I wouldn't be who I am today. I'm such a better person because of my alcoholism," I say emphatically.

"Really?" Bert tilts his head. "That's so interesting. You don't hear many people say that. Or, at least, *I* haven't heard many people say that, but I'm not in the recovery community. Maybe you *do* hear that fairly often in your community?"

"I do, yes, in the recovery community. I think it's because once you're able to get a few days sober and you start to clean up some things, you begin to realize all that you've learned from your addiction. And I learned to be more kind, more understanding, more patient, and more accepting. I learned I'm resilient, and that I'm much stronger than I ever thought I was."

"That's amazing, Charlie. I'm so happy to hear that," he says, his eyes beaming with pride.

"But enough about me. We know all about me—what's up in *your* life, dude? You're a professor in Switzerland, Bert! Can we just take a moment and realize how fucking amazing that is! Like, remember when we were smoking blunts, living in the fraternity house, oblivious to the world? Well, you weren't, but I sure was! I remember that Bert so well, and I feel so lucky that you're my friend! I'm so impressed with you!" I chortle.

"Easy now, it'll all go to my head," he jokes, grinning.

"But seriously, you're a European professor! The fanciest of us all," I laugh.

"It has been a lot of fun," he says coyly. "I didn't think it was gonna turn into this, but I'm so happy it did."

"I am, too! Do you think you'll teach in Zürich for a long time? I mean, do you plan on putting down roots here?"

He shuffles his body on the couch, bending his long legs to sit crisscross.

"Actually, about two days ago, I was offered an amazing position at a university in the Netherlands. So, I'll probably be heading up there sometime soon before the semester starts."

"Holy shit, Bert! The Netherlands! I'm not even sure what country that is, but I know it's cool!" I gush.

"Some people call it Holland, and it's where Amsterdam is," he giggles.

"Oh yes, Holland! That's what we called it in elementary school, I think? I always get the Netherlands and Norway confused in my brain. But Norway is part of Scandinavia, right? That's a place, right? Or do we not say that word anymore?" I ask quietly, frightened I've accidentally misspoken.

"I don't think Scandinavia is a bad word, Charlie," Bert chuckles. "And

THE FROG NO MORE

yes, Norway is part of Scandinavia, and the Netherlands is tucked between Belgium and Germany."

"Yes, okay," I say, straining to picture a map of Europe in my head. "Spain and France, and Germany's another big chunk," I mutter, holding my hands in the air to represent countries in my mind, "so it's somewhere in the middle of all that? Okay, got it. Kind of," I blush.

"I'm impressed," Bert tips his head.

"I like geography. I found that out in college—did you take that geography class with us? A bunch of our guys from Sigma Pi took the same night class, but I don't remember you taking it."

"No, but I remember you all taking it! That's where the kitten Westerlies Meowzer was found, wasn't it?"

"Oh, my lands! I have not thought of Westerlies Meowzer in *years*! And yes, we found him outside Pearson Hall during a break. That's why we named him Westerlies—we were learning about the westerlies wind," I guffaw. "Ah, memories. I think the professor even stopped class for a while that day, once we got back with Westerlies. She was a cool professor. I can't remember her name, but I really liked her."

"Didn't you and Dapp and Ben keep him for a while?" Bert asks.

"We did, for a few days, or maybe a week? Or maybe longer, I don't exactly remember. I know Mary P, Kelli, and Ashley took care of him for a bit. I feel like he slept with Dapp and Kelli for several nights, but I could have that wrong. I'm also fairly sure we made a bed and litter box for him in one of the closets of the Gussi room."

"Oh, wow! Mary P, Kelli, Ashley, and Gussi—*that's* all such a throwback!" he laughs.

"Right? Oh, our college friends. Oh, I love them all so much! Did you live in the Gussi room?"

"What a time, huh? And nope—I was always your roommate, remember?"

"Oh, duh! What an era!" I exclaim. "You know, that time of my life—the college days—it's actually something I've used to gauge my quality of life."

"What do you mean?" Bert asks curiously.

"College was one of the happiest times of my life. It even beats my childhood, which was pretty damn magical. But in college, I was openly gay, I was acting, and I had more friends than I'd ever had in my life—*straight guy friends*—that I wasn't scared of. I had straight guy friends that accepted me and made me feel like part of a group of guys. It was amazing! That meant *so much* to me because I always wanted straight guy friends. I always wanted to be included, you know? And we were constantly doing something fun, hell, class was even fun! It was just one big happy party for four years, and when it ended, I couldn't handle it. Of course, I couldn't see that at the time. And I realize how insanely privileged that sounds, but it's true.

"And when I had almost a year sober, it just kind of came to me that I hadn't been this happy since we were all running around in college. So then, I thought to myself, 'okay, why do you think this is?' And when it gets down to it, I think it's because I'm living in a way that's true to myself. I'm loving on myself, I'm encouraging myself, and I'm excited for myself. I lost all that after college ended, and rather than search for it, I decided to blame myself for losing it. I decided to punish myself for not being better prepared. Counterproductive, for sure, but I quickly learned to love *that,* and we all know how that turned out. But I'm talking about myself a lot again, and I'd really like to hear about you!" I smile sheepishly. "Are you dating anyone?"

Bert sighs, a sardonic grin animating his face.

"Oh, dating. Not at this moment, no. I was seeing a girl a while back, for a few months, but it kinda fizzled out. She was really wanting to take it to the next level, and I wasn't even sure if I was going to stay in the country. But I'd like to meet someone, it's just hard when you never know how long you're gonna be somewhere," he shrugs.

"Well, what about this job in the Netherlands? Do you think you'll stay there for a while?"

"Maybe. They do tenure differently over here, so who knows? I'd still like to travel some more, though."

"You should write a travel memoir!" I suggest excitedly.

"You know, I've actually thought about doing something like that," he confesses.

"Oh, it would be so good! You've lived in Turkey and Zürich, and been to so many places, you should seriously do it, Bert! And take it from me, you just have to make yourself sit down and start writing."

"I know, I know. I just need to make myself start, and then I'd probably be off and running," he laments.

"You're exactly right. I just had to make myself start, and then I fell in love. I'd help you out, too, with peer reviews and stuff like that. You really helped me when you reviewed a chapter of the first book, and I'd like to return the favor."

"Oh, wow, thank you!" he beams.

"For sure, bud," I yawn, sleep tugging at me. "Okay, I should probably go lay down. I'm delirious and I've been awake for like thirty-seven hours or something."

"Yes, go to bed, sleepy head," he says, stretching.

"Night, bud," I yawn again, plodding to his bedroom, where Anne and I will share his bed while he graciously crashes on the couch.

Bert, the consummate gentleman.

*****

The bells of midnight toll from the Swiss Church of Wengen, their tranquil ring echoing throughout the silent village and down to the valley. I leap the incline of the cobblestone street, land in a twirl, and grin. This is absolutely *phenomenal!*

"I am the luckiest sober gay boy in the world!" I breathe, marveling at the quaint church nestled snugly on the hill, small in comparison to the great cathedrals of Europe, yet still grand and awe-inspiring. It sits near the cliff's edge and overlooks the village of Lauterbrunnen, a nest of pin-dot lights fifteen hundred feet below. My eyes sweep across the mountains and valley, astonished. The cover of the night has darkened the landscape, casting an eerie, gothic glow about the village, quite different from the bustling, vibrant energy of the day. Although, I think I may prefer the stillness of the night over the hustle of the day.

Treading carefully and slowly, I let my fingers glide over the small stone wall leading to the church, and rest my palm on the wood of the immense front doors.

"Sanctuary," I chortle.

The door's venerable hinges moan as I press against the wood, firm and smooth as the stones of the wall, polished by centuries of hands, and especially dark against the white walls of the church. I turn on my heel and walk toward the edge of the cliff, passing the thatched steeple and stepping out onto a rocky crag jutting over the valley. Noises from Wengen whisper around me: a dog bark, the wind's roar in the mountains, a woman's laugh. The inky night sky is covered with shining white stars, a silver half-moon hiding behind the soaring mountain peaks. The air is crisp and cool, thinner than what I'm accustomed to, yet cleaner and sharper. I gaze over Wengen and Lauterbrunnen, straining to see the streets and alleys in the starlight.

"Isn't this amazing?" I utter, struck suddenly by an idea.

Chuckling softly to myself, I pull my phone from my pocket and click on the compass, locating East. Taking a quick breath, I swallow, a snicker twitching on my lips.

"I call upon the Watchtower of the East, the Guardians of—" I inhale sharply, rubbing my temples and racking my brain. "Oh, damn it, I can't remember! Something about Air, obviously, but what else? Okay, think about it, Charlie, you silly gay boy. Okay, no, but this is serious now! No, it is," I giggle. "It is. Okay. I call upon the Watchtower of the East and the Guardians of Air, Gemini, and Mercury—*there* it is! I've still got it! Yes!" I whoop quietly with delight, then clear my throat. "Hi, it's been a while, huh? I've certainly thought about you over the years, though. And I've definitely called out to you when I've been wasted and deranged. When I've been out of my mind with shame and depression. So, um, sorry about all that. I wasn't right in the head, you know how that goes.

"But, as I look out over the Swiss mountains and this beautiful, crystal-clear sky of stars, I want to say thank you. Thank you so very much for all that you've given me. Thank you for watching out for me. Thank you for listening to me, and giving me only what I could handle at the time. Thank you for knowing what I didn't know—what I suppose I couldn't know—about myself, and helping me find that. I have never taken my good fortune lightly, and know it was by your grace.

"You see, as I'm sure you know, I was very aware of my luck and good fortune during all those wicked times. I have always been acutely aware of my privilege and good fortune. And it has brought me lots of guilt over the years. I'm not trying to be demeaning in any way, or say that I had it easy—I didn't—but I know you were there. You had to be, or I wouldn't be standing here today, experiencing this amazing, once-in-a-lifetime trip. I know that in my bones. You've begun to answer questions I asked as a young boy on the hills of Bucksaw. Or, rather, I've begun to open my heart and listen to your message.

"And while I don't know what you have in store for me, I *finally* trust you. I trust that you know best and that you always have my best interest in mind, even if it doesn't feel like it. Damn, do I understand that *now*!" I chortle, tears streaming down my cheeks.

"And what a gift that is! To trust. I had no idea—and for some of the time, I *thought* I was trusting, but I can see now that I wasn't. I was just so mixed up and wanted to live life to the fullest so badly, and I was scared that I wasn't. But I was—I have been my whole life—you've seen to that. And I thank you! But anyways, I'm rambling. I'm overwhelmed with gratitude, and it's all your doing. I know I'm someone you are proud of, and that lifts me higher than any drug or drink ever could.

"So, thank you, Guardians. Thank you for dealing with all my horseshit over these long years and always taking care of me. I would be nothing without you."

A mellow breeze stirs the night air, and I breathe deeply, moving to a grassy knoll near the church. I lay on my back and stare at the night sky, bubbling with euphoria and love. There's nothing quite like knowing I'm exactly where I'm supposed to be. There's nothing quite like true friendship. Spending time with Anne on our flight across the Atlantic Ocean, watching part of *The White Countess*, feasting on airplane food, swimming in memories, and giggling, was nothing short of sublime. Simple, yet sublime. Vodka took this from me for many years, and it is a joy to have it once again. It was an absolute joy to sit in the living room of Bert's Swiss apartment, the three of us together again, chatting and chuckling. There was a time, in the not-too-distant past, when all of this would have seemed like a fairy tale. Me, visit Europe? What a stark raving mad idea, indeed!

But here I find myself, in the company of some of my oldest and dearest friends, traveling throughout Switzerland and France. It is an accomplishment—an achievement—so far removed from the realm of what I thought possible, I might *still* be in shock.

Spreading my arms out like an eagle, I savor the scent of pine and fresh, pure air. A cricket sings mournfully from the meadow beside the church, and I turn my head toward their tiny concert. *This* is life's purpose; I was mistaken in Italy as a young man. This is mindfulness and gratitude wrapped into one. *This* is what it's all about. Could I have appreciated this moment were it not for my alcoholism, though? Surely my plunge into darkness has enhanced my ability to recognize and honor the glory of the light?

"Oh yes, I do believe so," I murmur.

*****

"What about here?" I say, pointing to a portion of unclaimed grass. "We can take excellent pictures from here!"

"Perfect, Lassie!" Anne agrees, beaming.

Sawyer and I spread a blue and green quilt over the grass, positioning it for the best possible angle of the Eiffel Tower, while Anne unpacks our picnic of cheese, meat, and fruit. The night sky of Paris is starless, clouded with a foggy sepia glow, and the square patch of ground before the Eiffel Tower crawls with spectators eagerly awaiting its hourly light show. Once the clock strikes midnight, sparkly lights will dance across the Eiffel Tower, twinkling majestically for up to five minutes. On my last trip to Paris, I drank buckets upon buckets of wine before visiting the Eiffel Tower, and have vague memories of standing beneath its base and snapping a picture with my digital camera. I believe that picture is in a binder locked away in a storage shed, however, I'm not certain. Wine was my constant companion when I last

THE FROG NO MORE

visited Europe and I do not miss it in the slightest.

"Oh, I'm so happy we're doing this! And how amazing is it that we're in Paris around Bastille Day? This is probably going to be extra beautiful!" Anne gushes, settling onto the quilt.

I grab a slice of apple and smile at her. "This whole trip has been amazing, Lassie. Thank you so much for planning it and for all of your help!"

"Thank you so much for coming! I've had so much fun, and I'm so bummed you have to fly out tomorrow! Ugh!" she fans her face, staving off tears. "It just makes me sad that it's almost over."

"Awe, Lassie, it makes me sad, too! Wouldn't it be great if this trip could go on forever?" I bemoan.

"Right? This has honestly been one of my favorite trips. It's been so casual and relaxed," Sawyer agrees, nibbling on cheese.

"You're right, Sawyer. I should focus on the moment at hand, not worry about it ending! What's been your favorite part so far?" Anne asks, making a sandwich of meat and cheese.

"Probably when we went to Interlaken," Sawyer nods.

"Oh! The pictures y'all took there were breathtaking!" I say. "I wish I would have gone, but my neck was *killing* me that morning and I think I had jet lag, maybe?"

"Oh, you *for sure* had jet lag!" Sawyer says matter-of-factly. "I felt so bad for you, I could see it in your eyes, you just looked so tired and achy."

"Lassie, I'm so sorry about your neck and jet lag, but can I also say how proud I am of you for bouncing back to life in, like, five hours! Seriously, when we came back from Interlaken, you were like a new man!" Anne chuckles.

"Mind over matter. The old tricks of an alcoholic," I grin. "Nah, it's just that I refused to be down for very long! I think it was because I didn't sleep the first night, and we'd been doing so much. But I wasn't gonna miss anything else, so I took a hydration packet, rested, and then I sang the songs of my ancestors in the shower and felt much better."

"Songs of your ancestors?" Sawyer giggles.

"'I'll Make a Man Out of You' from *Mulan*!" I grin shyly. "I actually did sing that at the top of my lungs in the shower while y'all were gone. I think the steam and hydration packet and *Mulan* put me right back on course. And I'd say my favorite part was when we walked that long trail in Lauterbrunnen and then went into the waterfall. That blew my mind!"

"Oh, Lassie, I'm so happy it did! And I'm so happy *Mulan* helped you, too! Remember when everyone used to sing that song before every performance at Drury?"

"Yes!" I cackle. "And what was *your* favorite part, Lassie?"

"Hmm," she chews her bottom lip, contemplating. "I did love Interlaken, and Lauterbrunnen. I also loved our magical boat tour in the South of France."

"It really was magical!" I agree.

"Oh, and do you want to hear some scandalous gossip I stumbled upon on Instagram?" Anne whispers surreptitiously.

"Always!" Sawyer and I answer in unison, tittering.

"Remember the girl on our boat from Oregon?" Anne asks and we nod. "Well, I think she ended up staying on the boat with the tour guide, Yannick!"

I glance at Sawyer, her mouth agape.

"Oh, wow! Oh, that's wild! Well, good for her!" I clap, plucking a slice of meat from our picnic.

"Right?" Anne chortles. "I was on Yannick's Instagram, to see if there were any pictures of us snorkeling, and I noticed that there were pictures of the two of them having a moonlit, romantic dinner in the middle of the ocean on his boat. Like, how fun! A romance in France!"

"Dang! She's having a different kind of trip than I've had, 'cause I've just been super relaxed. This has been such a refreshing trip. It's been a trip of a lifetime," I declare, then spring to my feet. "Oh, look!"

A dazzling festoon of lights blooms over the Eiffel Tower and I guffaw with mirth, vowing to soak up this moment, a great ending for a great trip.

*****

Pausing *Stranger Things*, I lean my head against the large glass window of the Paris airport, Charles de Gaulle. My flight leaves in three hours, and I scroll through my phone, deciding to call my best friend from high school, my best

THE FROG NO MORE

friend for life, Devin. The phone rings twice before she answers.

"Hi, silly! It's early here!" she chortles sleepily.

"Oh, shit! It's barely six in the morning there, huh?"

"Yeah, but the dogs were already stirring. What're you doing?"

"Just sitting in the airport in Paris, waiting to board my flight."

"Fancy," she drawls playfully.

"Oh, yes, very fancy!" I giggle. "I've been here for two hours, eaten fairly decent McDonald's, and watched *Stranger Things*. Trashy American that I am. But Paris loves *Stranger Things*—they had the most amazing store and display on the Champs-Élysées."

"Oh, my God—what season are you on?" she asks.

"I'm on season four, and it's blowing my fucking mind! Like, I'm just sitting in this airport having this overwhelming experience with a TV show and Kate Bush. I'm also super emotional from the excitement and nostalgia of this trip and I feel, I dunno—I feel elated! I haven't slept much in the last week, either, so I might be slightly delirious." I muse.

"Sounds like you had a fun trip."

"It was such a great trip, I had so much fun!" I gush.

"What was your favorite part?"

"Switzerland. I think I might be in love with Switzerland. It's just so gorgeous—and last time, when we went in high school, I just remember it being snowy. Remember, we stayed at a hotel in the mountains and almost couldn't get the tourist bus up the entrance? I drank so much there, all my memories are fuzzy, but I remember riding in a ski lift with you and Alicia to a restaurant on top of a mountain, and Alicia said something really funny about her ass, and then being in that hotel with the massive dining room, getting drunk with people from Germany and France."

"Oh, wow, I had forgotten all about drinking with the people from Germany and France. Nick was actually having a conversation in French!"

"Yeah, I've thought about our trip a lot while being here. Before I flew out, when I was waiting at the airport in Kansas City, I was worried that this trip would feel different. That it wouldn't feel as exciting and new, since I'm older. I mean, the last time we went, we were at a very impressionable age, and I so wanted to feel that feeling again, of being in a foreign country, with an ocean between me and everything I've known. It's so exhilarating! I was terrified it wasn't going to feel that way, that it would just feel like traveling in the States, but that didn't happen. As soon as we touched down in Zürich, I felt the same tingly, excited feeling I felt the first night we went walking around London all those years ago. It was so reassuring."

"I know what you mean. When I went back, in college, I was worried it wouldn't be as exciting, but it was. But, um, I just gotta know—did you get lucky? Any flings with hot European boys? I know you were wanting to!"

"Oh, my gosh, no!" I giggle. "Damn it! I honestly didn't even try. I thought I was going to when we got to the South of France, but I never actually went through with it. I'm such a lazy slut. But damn did I see some fine-ass men on this trip! Especially in Switzerland. I swear everyone in Switzerland is a knock-out, they're all gorgeous. I even did a double-take for some of the women!"

"Well, dang it! I was really hoping you'd have a European fling!" Devin chuckles.

"Me, too! But oh well. Kept myself pure this go-round. Guess I'll have to come back again and slut it up another time."

"Rough life," she mutters. "Did you miss Klaus?"

I balk dramatically.

"Listen, I have missed that cat more than I knew was humanly possible. And you want to know how much of a lunatic I am? I literally whispered good night to him each night, with my eyes closed real tight, telling myself he could feel me saying it. I'm cracked in the head. But I *love* that little guy. And Anne and Sawyer both have cameras at their houses, so they could check on their cats, and I was so jealous! I have to get one of those first thing when I get home."

"Oh, no! I didn't know you didn't have a camera for him! Oh, how dreadful! It's hard leaving them, huh?" she says with empathy.

"Yes! I mean, I knew it was going to be tough because he saved my life and I'm super co-dependent with him. But damn! And then I'd be having so much fun throughout the day, and I'd remember him and feel guilty. I'm a fucking pro at feeling guilty, though."

"Nah, you sound pretty normal. We're all nuts about our animals nowadays."

"This is very, very true. But I'll let you go, just wanted to chat for a bit. We should plan a trip back here, though! So, think about that, and have a great day!" I chirp.

"Oh, that would be amazing! Alright, well, have a safe flight, and text me when you're back in the States. See you later!"

"Will do! Bye!" I reply, ending the call and pulling up a picture of Klaus. "Oh, buddy. Daddy will be home soon, and I'll never leave you this long again."

Blowing a raspberry with my lips, I click on Netflix and fall back into *Stranger Things*.

12

To 2023 & Beyond!

Winter 2023
Clinton, Missouri
Puerto Vallarta, Mexico
36 Years Old

Snow falls drowsily outside the living room window as Lorna plops on my checkered red and white chair, tucking her metal tumbler of water between her legs.

"Charlie freakin' Gray!" she smirks.

"Lorna freakin' Vickers!" I grin. "I'm so happy you're here at my house right now. It's been way too long!"

"It sure as hell *has*!" she cackles. "Oh, but I'm so happy to be here. It's *so good* to see you again, friend!"

"I know! I feel like it's been a *lifetime*, you know? Like—holy shit—my life's been batshit wild since we graduated high school, and I feel like parts of your life have been, too, and—wow! Here we sit. I'm so glad we both made it. 'Twas a dangerous journey."

"That's no shit," she laughs dryly.

"So, catch me up. Tell me about your life," I say, sitting across from her on my recliner. "I mean, you have kids!"

"I sure do! A girl and a boy, Tula and Remmy."

"Oh, I love their names!" I gush. "Tula and Remmy, so original and pretty!"

"Thanks," she beams, a proud mother. "They're my rocks, they're what got me through so much. If it weren't for them, there's no telling what would have happened to me."

"So, what *did* happen? I was still in college the last time we hung out, and then I sorta lost track of you. Well, I sorta lost track of *everyone*," I admit, glancing at the ground solemnly.

"Ah, no worries. I did, too. I got into meth real bad, just shooting and snorting it for days on end, and that lasted for about eight years or so. Living like that. Going from trailers to barns to cars to nothing.

"When I got pregnant with Tula, I cleaned up my act for a year and a half, but then I started drinking, of all fucking things. That turned into a helluva shit show, and then, not long after I started drinking, I got back onto meth again. I got pregnant with Remmy when Tula and I were living in a trailer without electricity or water. It was all busted up and in a field on Yost's land—"

"—holy shit, Lorna! *Yost's land!*" I gape.

"Oh yeah, Charlie, things got fucking *real*," she shakes her head. "I tried not to use or drink with Remmy, but I won't lie, I wasn't always sober, and thank God he turned out to be a perfect, healthy little angel." She rubs her eyes and rests against the back of the chair. "But, it was when I was about to lose them both that I looked at my life, and for the first time, I admitted that it was absolute bullshit. The way I was living was bullshit, and I had to stop it because only *I* could, and it wasn't fair to my babies. They sure didn't ask to have a dopehead, drunk-ass mother.

"So, I stopped. It was a *fucking nightmare*, and I wanted to crawl out of my skin and burn this hamlet of shit to the ground, but I made it. And my babies fought with me, they stood right beside me and fought off that old bullshit life, too, and I'm so proud to be their mom. I'm so proud of them," she smiles, simply and peacefully.

I swipe a tissue from the box and swallow. "Well, I'm a wreck! *Wow*! I'm genuinely so happy to hear every single word that just came out of your mouth, Lorna! I'm fucking *crying* right now, and I don't usually do that sober.

I'm so happy for you—I'm so proud of you! And you remembered 'hamlet of shit,'" I use my fingers as quotation marks, "and I can't even right now!"

"I see you haven't changed all that much," she jests.

"Nope!" I chortle tearfully. "Oh, this is so great. This is why moving back home, whether I wanted to or not, was actually the best thing that ever happened to me. Because of moments just like this."

Lorna kicks off her tennis shoes and pulls her legs onto the chair. "Where were you before you moved back?"

"California. And it was great until it wasn't anymore. I finished a program out there and had to move into a different sober house, and it was all kind of sudden and unexpected, so I started drinking again. It was such a mess. I'd just gotten a good job at a bank and was due to start in a week, but I said fuck it all, left the sober house, and started drinking and hanging out on the streets. I think I was experiencing some sort of mental breaking point in my life, but I haven't quite worked that one out yet.

"Anyways, yeah, I ended up right back here in Clinton, Missouri, as I'd always done before, but something changed this time. *I* changed this time." I say zealously, nodding.

"I get that. It had to be you making the change, or it was never going to happen."

"Exactly."

"And look at you now, Mr. Writer!"

"Oh, shit, yeah," I blush, scratching my ear.

"I'll be honest, I haven't read the second one yet, but I read the first one and it was amazing, Charlie. I'm so sorry you had to go through all of that, but it's so amazing that you did and that you survived."

"Thank you. Thank you very much. And I'm sorry you had to go through everything *you* went through! Hell, you've survived, too! More than me, you gave birth! Twice!"

"Oh, yes. For sure! But, when you think about it, we really should have seen it coming," she reflects quietly, slowly making eye contact with me. We remain stone-faced for a moment, then burst into a riot of laughter.

"The signs *really were* all there, weren't they?" I gasp between giggles.

THE FROG NO MORE

"All of them!" she says, wiping a tear from her eye. "Oh, man, yeah, we should have seen that coming."

"Oh, for sure. But, c'est la vie," I shrug.

"C'est la vie," she nods, sipping from her metal water bottle and tilting her head, her eyes inquisitive. "You got a boy?"

"I have Klaus," I answer coyly. "And right now, he's the only boy I need. What about you? You got a girl? A boy? Are you after both now?"

"Oh, hell," she tosses her head back, tickled. "Men were a weird phase of my life, but I'm so thankful for that phase because it gave me Tula and Remmy. But I dunno, I don't see a man playing a significant role in my love life, that's for sure. I'm much more comfortable with women. And much more attracted to women. Sadly, though, I don't have a girl right now, no. I was talking to one, for a while, but that sort of ended a couple of weeks back. And I'm so busy with the kids, it's hard to find the time to date."

"It's surreal, hearing you say that. Shit, we're getting so old!" I groan.

"No, we're not, we've just lived a lot of life," she retorts gently.

"That is a beautiful way of putting it, Lorna. I love that," I say.

"So why don't *you* want to date?" she presses.

"Oh, shit," I sigh, leaning back in the chair. "I've just never really dated, you know? For years, I was too busy drinking and running all over the country from one rehab to another—I never stopped long enough to actually think about dating. It wasn't a priority for me, and I guess that became my normal after a while.

"I'm sure there's some exploration I need to do when it comes to my aversion to dating and being in a relationship, but I dunno, maybe I'm just super selfish?" I chortle. "Being in a relationship takes time and work—I feel like I'd have to check in with someone all the time. I dunno, really. I'm sure the right guy could change all that. I mean, if Jack Wolfe suddenly fell into my life, I'd take back everything I've said and husband-up real fucking quick, but I seriously doubt that's gonna happen."

"Who's Jack Wolfe?" Lorna balks.

"An amazingly perfect actor who is perfect and amazing. And so beautiful, and perfect," I fawn, googly-eyed and twitterpated.

"Oh, my God, you're so gay," she chuckles, pulling her phone from her pocket. "But the look on your face when you talk about him—I've got to check this guy out."

"I'm telling you, he's amazing and perfect," I mutter feverishly.

"Oh, wow," she says, scrolling through her phone. "Yes, he is very easy on the eyes. Well, I wish you two the best."

"Oh? Thank you! A boy can dream, you know."

"For sure! But, um, buddy, do you think you might have some commitment phobia? I know you're a king of therapy, but it kinda sounds like you could be scared of commitment," she shrugs.

"Oh, definitely. Most certainly! And it's probably just the classic fear of the unknown. I've only been in a couple of committed relationships, and one of them was in rehab, so it's not like I have much experience. I think I'm scared of being co-dependent, too. 'Cause I'm stupid co-dependent with this cat," I say, grabbing Klaus as he saunters by and wrapping him in my arms. "This guy stole my heart."

"They do that," Lorna muses, rising from the chair to pet Klaus. "But he helped save you, so I'd say it's alright if you're co-dependent with him."

"Thank you, Lorna," I murmur.

"So, you're going to Mexico, huh? That should be exciting!" she says, ambling back to the chair.

"Yup, at the end of February, with my family. I'm really looking forward to it! It's beautiful where we're going, Puerto Vallarta. It's on the Pacific side. I've been there once before with them, and I managed to stay sober on that trip. The very first time I went with them, though, in 2017, we went to Playa del Carmen, on the Caribbean side, and I kept sneaking around to drink. It was awful. I enjoy traveling sober so much more."

"How *has* that been for you? Traveling sober? Was France hard? With all that great wine?"

"You know, I honestly never could tell the difference in wines. I mean, sure, I can tell the difference between red and white wine. But I couldn't tell you if I was drinking cheap red wine or expensive red wine, it all tastes the same to me. Which, I think, is kinda nasty, really. Like, corky-tasting and dry and bitter and just *not* refreshing at all. I used to say I loved red wine, but what I really meant was I loved getting blackout drunk. There's a difference, trust me," I chuckle darkly.

"Really? I loved white wines—I feel like a lot of them were refreshing, but I know what you mean about red wine. The headaches!"

"Maybe some of the whites, but otherwise, nasty," I cringe. "But to answer your question, traveling and staying sober has been super easy. I never really realized it until I was in Europe last summer, but I've literally traveled the world drunk, you know? I've been to England, France, Switzerland, Italy, Mexico, and all over the United States just drunk as a skunk! I've *done* it, you know? I've been drunk fucking *everywhere*! Maybe that's why it's easier? Because I've already done it? Or maybe it's because I don't want to drink anymore. I gave enough of my life to vodka. I gave way too much of my life to vodka, if we're being real. And I honestly feel like I've moved on from it.

"Now don't get me wrong, I'll never forget its power, I'll never forget what I let it do to me, how I fueled its power. But I never want to invite it back into my life. It's there, I know that—it'll always be there. But I refuse to engage with it any longer. I refuse to fall under its spell again. It shall bow to *my* will now, for I will no longer bow to it. And that just got super dramatic!" I giggle.

"No, I fucking liked it! And I know what you mean! For me, it's like, I know I could have meth like *that*," she snaps her fingers loudly, "if I wanted it. I know how easy it is to find it and fire up a bowl. But I also know how easy it is for me to keep living this fucking *amazing* life I've built for myself. They're both easy decisions, you know?"

"Okay, but I liked *that*, Lorna! I'm having a damn epiphany here! Like, at the end of the day, it really is an easy decision: do I want to better my life, or fuck everything up and get shitty blackout. 'Cause yeah, I could so easily go back to my old life—just like that," I snap. "And it's almost like knowing that makes the decision to stay sober easier."

"Took us long enough, huh?" she observes, deadpan.

I erupt in belly laughs as Lorna shakes her head. "Sure did!"

*****

"Wow, you've really saved Granny's plants, huh?" Trella remarks, motioning toward a fledgling poinsettia, surrounded by ivy, both reaching for the sun on a slim table beside my brown recliner.

"Yup! I think they just needed some water and love," I nod.

"She'll be so happy you were able to save them! You should take a picture and send it to her, it'll brighten her day."

"Oh, I should, shouldn't I? I'll put them on the coffee table and spruce them up a bit," I say.

"You've got such a green thumb, Bub," Trella chuckles. "You get that from your Grandpa Joe, 'cause your mom sure didn't have a green thumb, and I don't, either."

"I'm learning I got *a lot* of things from Grandpa Joe," I observe. "I'm starting to think I'm kinda like a carbon copy of him. We drank the same way—mainly vodka, guzzling it all day long until our poor bodies couldn't take it anymore. And I've thought about him *a lot* over these last couple of years, and there's one thought I keep circling around. Why do you think he wasn't able to stay sober?"

Sunshine pours through the window of my living room, pooling warmly on the gray carpet, where Klaus is sprawled on his back, passed out and peaceful. I nudge him with my toe and he yawns, stretches, then crawls onto Trella's lap. She sighs and scratches him in "his spot," between his shoulder blades.

"Well, he never took the time to honestly try and stay sober," she tilts her head, considering. "And he never did anything for *himself*. He never stopped drinking for *himself*. He'd quit for Mom, or he'd quit for work, or because someone in the family had shamed him. But he never quit because he wanted to. And he'd *always* drank, you know? He'd done it his whole life—since he was a young kid—and it's all he knew."

"Damn! I understand *that*! You know," I say, crossing my legs and leaning back in my squishy orange leather chair, "alcohol has been a part of my life since I was a kid, too. I'd say since about the age of ten. I hadn't realized it until right before I started writing the third book, but when I look as far back as I can remember, alcohol is there. It's right there, even at ten years old! Swiping abandoned cups of wine when I was little, sipping beer at nearly every fish fry, and drinking rum on trail rides. It's always been there. Isn't that wild?"

Trella nods, a stunned gleam in her eye. "I hadn't really thought of it until now, either. But you're right! We sure didn't make it very hard for you to find it."

"I think I would have found it either way. And even before Mom died, I would sneak those Zima drinks sometimes, and drink them really fast because it made me feel happy and loopy, and I liked it. I always liked the way alcohol made me feel. It never made me feel out of control, until the end. For years, though—well, shit, for decades—it made me happy and loopy. I drank after Mom died because I was searching for those feelings of elation, freedom, escape, and happiness. Obviously, I didn't know that at the time, but looking back, I can see that my alcoholic patterns began *way* before Mom died."

"Huh," Trella clucks, relaxing into my worn brown recliner, Klaus snoozing on her lap obliviously. "When do you think all that started?"

"At ten, definitely. I mean, I wasn't drinking all the time, like an alcoholic, until my early twenties, but I was drawn to alcohol in the same way an alcoholic is—it had a power over me—from a very young age.

"I was fully aware of alcohol by ten. I understood there were different kinds, liquor was the strongest, and I liked sweet red wine and Zima the best. I used to love to sneak them at parties in the pavilion. I don't think I ever got fully drunk until after Mom died, though. Maybe I did and I don't remember it, but I'm pretty sure I remember the first time I got *drunk* drunk," I swallow. "It was at Granny Norma Jean's house, shortly after Mom died, and I chugged five beers, one right after the other. It honestly kinda hurt my stomach, but I for sure got drunk.

"And then, for the next few months, I would drink Southern Comfort and Coke, alone, at our house on Antioch. And I didn't always get drunk—sometimes it was only a drink or two. But sometimes I would get drunk. One time, I drank so much that I got sick all over the bathroom, cleaned it all up, took a shower, and faked sick so Dad and Brod would leave me alone. I mean, holy hell! That's behaving like an alcoholic at thirteen and fourteen years old!" I gape.

"Yeah, I remember that year on Antioch after Brenda died," Trella says with a faraway look. "I remember wondering if you were drinking. I never knew for sure, but I wondered. I've always wondered about you and alcohol."

"Well, that makes sense, since it's always been a part of my life."

"Do you still feel like it's a part of your life now?"

"I do, yes. But it's not a part of my life in the way it once was. I'm not foolish enough to think I've cured my alcoholism. I struggled for way too long—it held me down too long—I know there's *no curing* what it can do to me, how it can take me over in an instant. It will always be a part of me, it will always be there. That doesn't mean I want it, though. And I understand it now like never before. I understand *myself* now like never before. I understand that I am genetically pre-disposed, and that I absolutely loved being fucking hammered, you know? And what's even better is that I understand *why* I loved being hammered. I *finally* get it now, after all these years. I get it! And there's so much freedom in that. There's so much forgiveness, too."

"What do you think did it for you?"

"My soul wouldn't tolerate being smothered by vodka any longer. That sounds dramatic, but I am dramatic. And it's the truth. I mean, you know all about 'good Charlie' and 'bad Charlie,' and that's what it was. Good Charlie finally beat bad Charlie. I think it's that way for a lot of people. Their soul, the truth of who they are, finally wins out. There came a point when I recognized being angry and full of shame wasn't helpful, it wasn't deserved, and I was able to say fuck it all. Fuck everything you did, Charlie! Yeah, it was terrible, and I hate that I did it, but it's done. And I survived. I may have lost most of my dignity, but I survived. Dignity can be repaired, but a life lost cannot.

"And I think that's what did it. I gave myself the tiniest bit of forgiveness, and that's all the power good Charlie needed to overthrow bad Charlie. And let me tell you, as soon as good Charlie was able to come through, he gave bad Charlie quite the ass-whopping. Which sounds absurd and ludicrous and maybe like I should talk with a psychologist, but you know what I mean," I grin.

"I most certainly do. And, when I think back on it, I know right when good Charlie really started to surface."

"You do?" I ask, prickling with excitement.

"Oh, think about it! It was about the same time you got Klaus, maybe a little before," she says, softly rubbing his ears. "You had started to ease up on yourself. You'd started to relax. You'd been sober a couple of months, and as soon as you brought Klaus into your apartment, I knew you were *really* doing better. I knew you weren't as scared as you had been because you allowed yourself to keep him. You gave yourself permission. And at the time I didn't want to say anything, but I thought to myself that it was a really good sign. You were trusting yourself again, which meant you were forgiving yourself, too."

"Oh, wow, you are one hundred percent right, and I don't know if I ever would have realized that! Yup, it would have been the end of September in 2020, when I really started to forgive myself and relax. I like how you phrased that because it's exactly what I did. I relaxed in life. I relaxed in sobriety. I caught my fucking breath!" I chuckle.

"That's no joke!" Trella agrees, laughing with me.

"And thank the stars! I can't imagine still being out there. I can't imagine not being Klaus' dad or being around to be present as an uncle in Nash's life. It makes me sad if I think about relapsing. I'm so happy to have my family back and be an active and useful member of it, and it's so sad to think how that would all fall away if I were to drink. It used to make me scared and make my body ache, but now it makes me sad because I think of what would happen to Klaus or the fact that Nash and Scottie wouldn't know me. Addiction is such a sad disease when you really get down to it. It's easy to be mad at it, but I think most of us are really just sad at it."

"But it never has to happen again, Bub, if you don't let it," Trella offers as Klaus rises from her lap, jumps to the ground, and arches his back.

"This is very true!" I agree. "And I'm so relieved to finally be at a place in my life where that decision is a choice for me. There was a time when it wasn't. For most of my twenties, it was beyond a choice or a decision."

Klaus headbutts me affectionately, pawing at my feet.

"Oh, you little poopbutt! Did you get the munchies after that big nap? Do you need a snack, little buddy? C'mon, let's get you a snack."

"He's got you tied around his little claws," Trella jests.

"He sure does," I giggle. "But I wouldn't want it any other way."

"Me either, Bub! Me either," she smiles.

*****

The morning sunlight beams upon the right side of my face, warm and bright. I stare at my porthole-themed mirror, tilting my head to the side and watching the light refract in my blue eyes. Klaus rolls on his back, soaking up the sunlight streaming through the front storm door, and yawns sleepily.

"You're so darn cute, do you know that? Gonna take you a nappy-nap, buddy?" I murmur, turning back to my reflection. "You take you a nappy-nap, buddy, and Dad's gonna stand here and talk to himself in this mirror for a bit. I haven't done this in *months*, and for some reason, I feel very compelled to do it right this moment."

Studying my reflection in the mirror, I sigh.

"You're aging, boy. You're going to be thirty-seven in a couple of months. Thirty-seven! Why does that sound so old? It's not—it's just—damn! It got here fast! Life moves so fast. You don't realize that when you're young, Klaus," I glance at him, lounging and watching me as I prattle.

"At least, *I* didn't realize it. I guess I thought my twenties would last forever. I guess I always thought something magical would happen and change my life forever. Not magic like *Potter*, but that someone or something would come along and whisk me off my feet and into another life, an exciting life.

"And you know, I guess that *did* happen, didn't it? Vodka came right along and whisked me off on a journey of absolute madness. Oh, Klaus, if you could have known me then. Thankfully, though, you didn't. It was such an odd, strange time. But, you know, I *am* grateful for it all. I really am. I do wonder, though, what my life would have looked like had I not become a raging alcoholic.

"Like, I wonder if I would have met someone? Would we have gotten married? Would we have had kids? Would I have *wanted* kids? I remember a time, around 2015 or so, when I thought I *did* want a kid. I wanted a little girl.

THE FROG NO MORE

I wanted to adopt a little girl, and it would be the two of us against the world! I wanted to give her the upbringing and chances that I never got. I wanted to make sure she didn't grow up fractured. But that all sort of faded away the longer I stayed in my addiction. I do still think about her sometimes, though. I sure do.

"And I imagine my life as a husband, too. It's a little fantasy I like to play out sometimes, of me meeting the man of my dreams. He's taller than me, with light brown skin, curly black hair, almond-shaped dark brown eyes, and plump lips. He doesn't care for alcohol or drugs, enjoys nature and being outdoors, and has a bubble butt from hiking," I chortle at Klaus. "Listen, it's my dream guy, okay? Why not go all out?

"And he loves me so much—like, he's so enamored with me, he thinks I hung the moon. And I feel the exact same way about him. We're forever infatuated with each other. That's not too much to ask for, is it? I mean, I feel like *I'm* a damn good package, and I deserve the man of my dreams. But do I really want him, you know? Like, do I *really* want him forever, or do I just want him for a few weeks?"

I gaze at myself, searching my eyes.

"Do I want a life partner? I honestly don't think I do, but I don't know if that's just something I've conditioned myself to say out of fear. What if Lorna really was getting close to the truth of it? What if I do have a phobia of commitment? Is it because I'm afraid to fall in love and become co-dependent? Did my co-dependency with vodka scar me so deeply that I'm afraid to let anything or anyone get that close again?

"No—I've let *you* get that close, Klaus. I'll let people in, but probably only on my terms, huh? And a cat is not a life partner, Charlie. It's a companion, oh yes, but it's not a life partner. Shit. I'm scared to death of being co-dependent, aren't I? And I'm afraid of someone having power over me—I'm afraid of falling in love. Is that why I let go of Aiden? And probably Jayce, too? I loved them fiercely and it frightened me—I have an intense phobia of being in a relationship, of being co-dependent, and I need to work on that. But you were co-dependent on vodka, Charlie! Were you scared of being co-dependent on vodka *and* Aiden? Are you just scared? *Damn it*! This is all so confusing! Oh,

I *knew* the work wasn't done yet! I *knew* it was going to get more layered and complex!"

I rub my face and stretch my neck with a groan.

"I'm scared because I know the first time I fall in love, sober, I'm going to fall harder than I did with Aiden or Jayce. I'm going to fall so freaking hard in love because I've never really experienced that. I've never *really* experienced falling in love and being in a stable relationship while being sober. I was always drunk or using other drugs. Or running from myself. It will be my first time *truly* falling in love. Shit, no pressure there!

"And *that's* why I'm frightened of it. I'm putting all this pressure on it, I want it to be perfect and magical and exactly like a romantic comedy. But it's not going to be like that, and I'll have to cope with that. Oh, my God, though—you're so dramatic, how are you going to handle a break-up? Will you relapse? Will you use it as an excuse to relapse? Will it break you into pieces?"

My blood chills and I swallow dryly.

"Will I, though?" I whisper, my thoughts suddenly frantic and frenzied. "Surely not. If I've learned anything from all of this, it's that I'm much stronger than I think I am. And I seriously doubt future Charlie would crumble to pieces and relapse over a boy!

"Oh, shit!" I gasp, clamping my hand to my mouth. "That's pride and fear puffing you up! Those are lies that you just said, Charlie! You *know* how dramatic you are—you literally *just* said it! You know you'll be crushed and wallow in misery and despair for weeks! Okay, let's get a grip, you're sort of spiraling," I point a finger at myself. "Let's get back on track and focus on what you can control."

Shaking out my arms, I inhale a long, deep breath and count to four. Keeping my eyes closed, I take another calming breath through my nose and slowly open my eyes.

"Alright. I made a vow once, ages ago, that I would take care of myself no matter what. And I've held up my end of that vow excellently. Sure, I went through some shitty times, but I *always* took care of myself. There were times when it didn't seem like I was, but I was, on some level, or I wouldn't be standing here today. So remember that before you spiral out of control. Remember that you've always had your own back. You've always got your Guardians with you. You're a good person, Charlie Gray, and I give you permission to fall in love one day. I give you permission to fall absolutely head over heels in love one day. And if you get your heart broken, and shit hits the fan, well, we'll handle that when we get there, won't we? But you can't *not* live your life because you're scared. That's nonsense. You've read way too much of John Locke to think like that, and know much better than to deny yourself the chance of experiencing life and love!"

I chuckle loudly and drum my fingers on my cheeks.

"Oh, Klaus. Love will happen when it's supposed to, huh? I can wait. And at least I stayed sober for a year before thinking about dating, right? 'Course, I don't know if that necessarily matters all that much. I think it's more important that I listen to my instincts in sobriety. My gut—my heart—knows what's right for me and when. I've learned it's very beneficial for me to trust in my instincts, and nurture them. My journey to sobriety helped sharpen my instincts. I'm *really* healing, aren't I? I'm healing myself. Tackling fears and facing secrets I've kept from myself. I tell you, bud, I'm a full-time job. But it's so worth it."

He blinks from his yellow rug and licks his chops.

"And I seriously think we need to have a discussion about your addiction to treats. I know that look you're giving me right now, silly boy. You want a treat. Good Lord, what have I created?" I mutter with a cackle.

*****

The red and golden sun is a blazing flame of light on the horizon of the Pacific Ocean, slowly gobbled up by the endless water as it sets. I bury my feet in the coarse sand of Puerto Vallarta and rest my copy of *Violin* by Anne Rice on my towel. A warm breeze flows over the beach, carrying the scent of salt water and citrus. Mist hovers amid the mountain peaks across the bay. Closing my eyes and listening to the crashes of the waves, I relax my shoulders and allow my thoughts to drift.

Is this not the power you always dreamed of?

A voice whispers in my mind.

In this last year alone, you've lived the life you dreamed of as a young boy in Florence all those years ago. Do you remember the joy of life you felt while walking the streets of Rome? Well, it's happening again. Don't you see that? You've released yourself from your own internal prison. You freed yourself, you silly boy!

A smile tugs at my lips and I open my eyes, gazing at the greenish-blue color of the waves, which swiftly curl into whitecaps as they invade the silken shore. The voice is my own, it is my soul, and it speaks the truth. I have found my power. I have found purpose.

Over the course of my life, the greatest lesson I have learned thus far is to live in the moment in a loving and appreciative manner. I spent too many years agonizing over the past or tripping out about the future, too many years worrying and fretting for absolutely no reason. I forgot life is precious. I forgot life is what I make of it. I forgot myself.

But you have found yourself now!

And I have learned what matters to me. I have learned what is *truly* important. By struggling with the death of my mom, the fear of my sexuality, my confusion about religion, and the disease of alcoholism, I grew to understand what makes life worth living. It is the love I feel for my family and friends, the joy and peace I feel in their company. It is holding my nephew and watching him sleep, knowing he is safe in my arms. It is laughing and relaxing with those dearest to me. It is snuggling with Klaus on a rainy day, absorbing his unconditional love.

I feel exceptionally lucky and honored for the privilege of learning these lessons, as well. I am eternally grateful my soul refused to wither and yield to the trauma of my past. Heeding my dad's advice from long ago, a part of my mind never gave up on me: it was not frightened by my self-sabotaging thoughts or the brutality I put myself through, for it was capable of seeing the bigger picture. It knew a greater truth. It is the part of me that always understood I am not a "bad" person; I had merely placed myself in a position of hurdling over one bad experience after another, and while my experiences educated me, they do not necessarily define me. There is no reason whatsoever for me to define myself as a failed, wannabe actor who became a washed-up alcoholic. Life is too short for such utter nonsense.

Nowadays, I find it much nicer to define myself by my relationships with my family and friends, and my contributions toward the enlightenment and comfort of humankind. Upon becoming sober, I wanted nothing more than to repair the damage I had heaped upon my loved ones, and to share my story of personal redemption. During my active addiction, I longed to be connected with my family and friends, but vodka had built an impenetrable wall, enclosing me in a cell of self-inflicted torture and shame. It was my first mission to dismantle that wall, brick by brick, and in the process, reconnect with those I had shut out for over a decade. My second mission was to find a way of sharing my journey so that other alcoholics and addicts, and *their* families and friends, would no longer feel alone, wrong, or confused.

It is not my ambition to offer a "cure" for addiction or a "how-to" for recovery, as I do not believe the first even exists. These have never been intentions of mine, however, I do sincerely hope my story can be used as a guide for discovering to trust and love oneself. I *very much hope* my zany chronicles provide comfort and a chuckle when they are needed most. My journey taught me I have the power to look in the mirror and stand up for myself. I have the power and the right to love myself, no matter how low I may have fallen. I have the power to look in the mirror and be proud of the man I am. *I* have the power. *I do*. And I am most certainly, *by no means*, unique in that regard. I hope to help spread this message—I hope to help you find *your* power. I hope to help you see the light within yourself, for it shines brightly, and it shines mightily.

And in case no one has told you today: I *know* you are worthy, you are not alone, you *are not* wrong, and *you can recover*. I *know* this in my heart!

Charlie & The Frog
written
October 24, 2020 — May 10, 2023

About the Author

Charlie Gray is a recovering alcoholic sharing his experience of addiction, relapse, and sobriety in his quit lit trilogy *Charlie & The Frog*. Living eleven brutal years as a high-functioning alcoholic, he attended a plethora of treatment centers, detox facilities, psychiatric wards, hospitals, and sober houses across the United States. Fifty-four, to be exact, but who's counting? His story offers unique insight into the method and mind of a chronically relapsing alcoholic, and the tools necessary to combat such an affliction.

Charlie resides in his quaint hometown in Missouri, with his family, friends, and cat, Klaus. These days, he can usually be found searching for epic, inspiring moments, enjoying life in sobriety, and writing his debut novel, *The Phantom Maverick*.

You can connect with me on:
- https://www.atleastimnotthefrog.com
- https://www.facebook.com/atleastimnotthefrog
- https://www.instagram.com/hismajestycharles3rd
- https://www.tiktok.com/@atleastimnotthefrog
- https://www.youtube.com/@charliemgray

Also by Charlie Gray

Charlie Gray is the author of the quit lit trilogy *Charlie & The Frog*.

At Least I'm Not The Frog: A Zany Memoir of Alcoholism & Recovery

This memoir chronicles the escapades of aspiring actor and writer Charlie Gray, his downward spiral into a vodka bottle, and his profound realizations about life, family, friends, booze, trauma, and relapse as a now-recovering alcoholic. Beginning with his graduation from Drury University, this book follows Charlie's journey across twelve states, where he's exposed to the glittering underbelly of an addictive lifestyle through his stints in multiple rehabs, detoxes, sober homes, and psychiatric wards. It is with these zany, visceral, and illuminating stories that he weaves a message of growth and authenticity. His dreams were faded, smashed by the stain of vodka, yet he found a way to lift himself from those depths.

Charlie provides a candid tale for those who feel they're forever doomed to be addicted, forever doomed to be in search of their identity and dignity. *Those gross, cringe-inducing things you've done in your addiction?* He's done them, too. You're not alone. You're not wrong. You can recover.

The Frog's Bottle: A Zany Recollection of Relapse & Rehab

Once again, Charlie Gray has lost control, spending his days drunk on vodka and facing staggering legal troubles. In *The Frog's Bottle*, the second in his trilogy of quit lit memoirs, Charlie finds himself trapped by his old nemesis, relapse. With his fourth arrest for a DUI, the possibility of prison looming, and the terror of knocking at death's door stirring in the back of his mind, Charlie admits himself to his fifth rehab in two years, Meadowlark Renewal, a quaint residential treatment center in Kansas. Yet, it is as though fate perceived this, and therefore thrust together an extraordinarily tortured group of patients, as his time at Meadowlark proves to be a *most profound* experience. From felons to suburban grandmothers, Charlie spends 33 days among "his people," all the while learning, growing, falling in love, and unearthing disturbing truths he had avoided for nearly a decade.

Although the question remains: will his stay at Meadowlark be the final piece in his sobriety puzzle? Will he *finally* be able to maintain sobriety, or fall victim to the same mistakes of his past?

Made in the USA
Columbia, SC
09 June 2023

2f6d3fb5-1f9b-4859-b74d-a0c6a6d4b904R01